when i was a girl

Based on the WE: Women's
Entertainment Network series
WHEN I WAS A GIRL

Text for this book comes from interviews
conducted by Lucky Duck Productions/WE

when i was a girl

edited by
alison pollet

with an introduction by
linda ellerbee

POCKET BOOKS
New York London Toronto Sydney Singapore

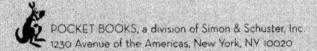
POCKET BOOKS, a division of Simon & Schuster, Inc.
1230 Avenue of the Americas, New York, NY 10020

ISBN: 978-0-7434-8064-2   ISBN: 0-7434-8064-3

First Pocket Books trade paperback edition September 2003

10 9 8 7 6 5 4 3 2 1

Manufactured in the United States of America

For information regarding special discounts for bulk purchases,
please contact Simon & Schuster Special Sales at 1-800-456-6798
or business@simonandschuster.com

A portion of
the proceeds
from this book
will be donated to

when i was a girl . . .

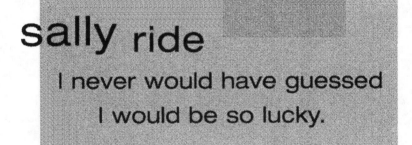

dee dee myers
I always had an answer and
I always had an opinion.

sally ride
I never would have guessed
I would be so lucky.

candace bushnell
I saw people
the way they really were.
I had no illusions.

ellen degeneres
I dreamed of being happy.

marian wright edelman
I loved life, wanted to
do everything and be
everything.

wendie malick
I wasn't sure I wanted
to become a woman.

acknowledgments

AMC NETWORKS

Katie McEnroe

Tom Barreca

Ed Henrich

WE: WOMEN'S ENTERTAINMENT

Martin von Ruden

Jeff Eisenberg

Lee Heffernan

Jennifer Geisser

Jennifer Robertson

Kimberly Iadevaia

Annmarie Volz

Ilene Richardson

Jesse Kasendorf

Christy Schmitt

Brad Mintz

Theresa Patiri

LUCKY DUCK PRODUCTIONS

Katherine Drew

Rolfe Tessem

Kathleen Murtha

Carolin Ehrenburg

Wally Berger

Jeff Gray

GIRLS INC.

Joyce Roché

acknowledgments

Alison Pollet gratefully acknowledges:
Christina Boys, Amanda Ayers, Liate
Stehlik, Donna O'Neill, Sybil Pollet,
Barbara Lichtman, Anita Sarno, Bayla
Cornell and the Fall River girls, Norma
Lesser, Ruthie Charles, Kate Aurthur and
Laura Kightlinger; and sends special
thanks to Estelle Pollet, a great person
and total knockout, now and when she
was a girl.

conten

ction

stumbling onto
our paths

Think back.

How far can you go? Four? Three? Two years old?
What do you remember? A toy? A dress? A pet? A day?
Close your eyes and imagine your girlhood bedroom.
What do you see? What songs did you sing and who sang
them to you? What did you believe in? Santa Claus? The
Tooth Fairy? Monsters under your bed?

When did you start to believe in *yourself?*

It's been said that memory is the portable little
library we all carry with us. In this book, as in life, it's the
details of memory that count, details that, when added
up, amount to something women share. It's clear that
many of the most powerful connections among women
are rarely documented in history books. Emotional ties
connect women. They are the ties that bind us, move
us—and often make us double over with laughter.

Call them the connections of the heart. This book is about those connections.

Here's how it happened. Rolfe Tessem (partner in business and in life) and I own Lucky Duck Productions. We produce television shows. In 2002 Marty von Ruden, executive vice president and general manager, and Jeff Eisenberg, vice president and executive in charge of production for WE: Women's Entertainment, asked us to collaborate on a television special. Because the "motto" of WE is "The Space We Share," we thought it would be good to celebrate something *all* women share on a personal level.

But what, exactly?

We weren't all the same race or religion—or age. We didn't all share the same politics or professions. We weren't all mothers. We weren't all married. Or single. We didn't all love the same kinds of men (or women) or go to the same kinds of movies or laugh at the same things. We didn't all look alike or dream alike. Apart from the perfectly obvious physical attributes of gender, what was it that all women shared?

We tried imagining a dinner party. If you could invite the most remarkable and diverse group of women to a dinner party—women who had followed different paths, and had succeeded in the arts, politics, literature, sports, science, business, activism—what was the one thing they would have in common? The answer proved to be, as answers often are, monumentally simple. That is, once we thought of it.

At one time or another all those women—indeed, all women—were little girls.

And so we put together a television special about defining moments in girls' lives. It included personal stories from some of the country's most recognized and distinguished women, stories that were individual and unique, but when told, spoke to, and collectively demonstrated, the shared experience of all girls.

That television special was called "When I Was a Girl."

We knew we were on to something when two things happened almost immediately. One, the women featured in the show told us how much they enjoyed the experience (said Candice Bergen, after telling us the story of an elaborate funeral her family held for a beloved pet turtle, "I've *never* been asked questions like these"). Two, when we showed the program to groups of women, at the end of it, they began talking, not about the program, but about their own experiences as girls.

And so *When I Was a Girl* became a series.

The series regularly catapults women back to an era, a milestone—a moment when they learned something about themselves. Of course not all memories were funny or funereal (not everybody's pet turtle got a five-star send-off)—but they were all telling.

Ann Curry, news anchor for *The Today Show,* said the thing she most treasured from her childhood was the dictionary her father gave her when she was twelve. She said he told her, "These words will open the world for you."

"And," said Ann, "they did."

Novelist Anna Quindlen said she wanted to speak up for nuns, because four nuns changed her life: her favorite nun; the nun who hated her; the nun who expelled her; and Sister Rita, the nun who led her to become a writer.

Opera singer Denyce Graves spoke of how a fluke in the weather gave her something to believe in, and a confidence she didn't have before that. "I remember the kids on the other side of the street thought they were better than us. And then one day it rained. But it only rained on their side of the street. I thought that was magic."

I guess it *is* rather like being invited to a wonderful dinner party with some of the world's most interesting women. Or little girls, as it were.

So sit down. Open the book. Join the party.

Think back. How far can *you* go . . . ?

One last note before you begin: Speaking for Lucky Duck Productions and WE, I want to say that this series has become a source of great pride, not to mention pleasure. It allows us to continue learning about the infinite variety of women's experiences—and what that means to all of us (yes, men too). And it really could not have been accomplished without the dedication, talent, and hard work of many people, including Rolfe, Marty, and Jeff (guys so smart they might have been women), but most especially that of Katherine Drew, vice president of development for Lucky Duck Productions, an uncommonly fine and creative woman I'd love to have known when she was a girl.

—linda ellerbee
may, 2003

when i was a girl . . .

rita moreno

I was a tiny little person with very curly hair, big dark eyes, and little matchstick legs. I was, in every sense of the word, a Latina. I whipped, I laughed, and it was always dramatic. I was loud, I was raucous, I was rowdy, and I cried. I'm a crier.

ann curry

I was physically strong,
big-boned, athletic, jumping off
of furniture, confident, curious,
and ready to tackle the world.

michelle rodriguez

I always wanted to get into things,
talk to strangers, and wander away
from my mother in the supermarket.

pants

GILLIAN ANDERSON

Golden Globe, Emmy Award, and Screen Actors Guild Award winner, Gillian Anderson found fame as Agent Dana Scully in the long-running television series *The X-Files*. Her film credits include *The X-Files* (1998) and Edith Wharton's *The House of Mirth* (2000). She most recently appeared onstage starring in Michael Weller's play, *What the Night Is For*.

INDIA.ARIE

R&B singer India.Arie is a founding member of the Atlanta-based artists' collective Groovement/Earthseed. The group's first independently released CD led to Arie's inclusion in *Lilith Fair* (1998) and helped launch her music career. In 2000 Motown released her debut album, *Acoustic Soul*, which was followed up with *Voyage to India* (2002). In 2002 she was nominated for a Grammy Award.

CANDICE BERGEN

Candice Bergen's career has spanned from high fashion model to star of her own television sitcom. Playing the title character in the sitcom *Murphy Brown* for ten years earned her five Emmy awards and sparked public debates throughout the country. Most recently she costarred in a remake of the film *The In-laws* (2003).

SANDRA BERNHARD

Sandra Bernhard, comedian, actress, vocalist, and writer, has starred on stage, in film, and on television. Both her one-woman shows, *Without You I'm Nothing* (off-Broadway/1988, as a film/1990) and *I'm Still Here . . . Damn It!* (Broadway and as a film/1998), received critical and audience acclaim. She has appeared in several films including *The King of Comedy* (1983) and *Truth or Dare* (1990), had a recurring role on the sitcom *Roseanne* (1991–97), and has been featured as a guest star on *Will and Grace* and *Ally McBeal*. In 2003 she returned to television with her own talk show, *The Sandra Bernhard Experience*.

ELLEN BURSTYN

Award-winning actress Ellen Burstyn has appeared in numerous films, her own television program, and on stages throughout the world. Her performance in *Alice Doesn't Live Here Anymore* (1974) earned her an Academy Award, and she won a Tony for the Broadway production of *Same Time, Next Year* (1975). She served as president of the Actors' Equity Association from 1982 to 1985, as coartistic director of the Actors Studio from 1982 to 1988, and in 2000 became the organization's president.

CANDACE BUSHNELL

Candace Bushnell is best known for her novels *Sex and the City* and *Four Blondes*. She has been a contributing writer and producer on the hit series *Sex and the City*, based on her novel. In addition she has written columns for the *New York Observer* and is a contributing editor for *Vogue*. Bushnell's newest novel, *Trading Up*, is due to be released this year.

JOAN CHEN

Actor, director, and producer Joan Chen made her film debut at the age of fourteen in *Xie Jin's Youth*. Three years later she starred in the film *Little Flower*, a role that garnered her a Best Actress Prize at the Hundred Flowers Awards. She made her American film debut in *Dim Sum: A Little Bit of Heart* and has since appeared in many films, including *The Last Emperor* and *Heaven and Earth*. Chen made her directorial debut with *Xiu Xiu: The Sent-Down Girl* (1998), and in 1999 directed the film *Autumn in New York*.

ANN CURRY

Ann Curry began her career in television news as a reporter and anchor before becoming an NBC correspondent and anchor of the network's early morning program, *News at Sunrise*. Her current position as news anchor for *The Today Show* and correspondent for *Dateline NBC* has earned her several awards and recognitions. A four-time winner of the Golden Mike Award, Ann Curry has received Associated Press Certificates of Excellence, an NAACP Award for Excellence in Reporting, and an Emmy Award.

ELLEN DEGENERES

In 1994 standup comedian Ellen DeGeneres starred and executive-produced the television series *Ellen*. In April 1997 the character DeGeneres played became the first to openly acknowledge her homosexuality on television. She has appeared in many films, including *The Love Letter* and *Ed TV* (both 1999). She also starred in HBO's *If These Walls Could Talk 2* (2000). Her latest endeavor is a television talk show launching in 2003.

ILLEANA DOUGLAS

Actress Illeana Douglas made her film debut in the 1987 comedy *Hello Again* and has since appeared in many feature films, among them *GoodFellas* (1990), *Cape Fear* (1991), *Household Saints* (1993), *Quiz Show* (1994), *Grace of My Heart* (1996), *Ghost World* (2000), and *The Kiss* (2003). She guest-starred on the television shows *Law and Order: Special Victims Unit* and *Six Feet Under*.

MARIAN WRIGHT EDELMAN

Advocate and author Marian Wright Edelman served as the legal defense fund attorney for the National Association for the Advancement of Colored People from 1963 to 1968. She founded the Washington Public Policy Research Center as well as the Children's Defense Fund. Her achievements have earned her the Albert Schweitzer Humanitarian Prize, Heinz Award, and MacArthur Foundation Prize Fellowship, and in 2000 she received the Presidential Medal of Freedom and the Robert F. Kennedy Lifetime Achievement Award.

MELISSA ETHERIDGE

Singer/songwriter Melissa Etheridge has sold more than twenty-five million albums worldwide, and earned two Grammy awards and ASCAP's Songwriter of the Year Award with the help of such hit singles as "I'm the Only One," "I Want to Come Over," and "Come to My Window." In 2000 she opened the Democratic Convention, and in 2002 organized and performed at the Human Rights Campaign's *"Equality Rocks."*

CHRIS EVERT

Tennis champion Chris Evert has won three Wimbledon championships, seven French singles championships, six U.S. Open titles, and the Australian Open twice. She is the founder of Evert Academy and appears as a frequent commentator on professional tennis broadcasts.

EDIE FALCO

Best known as Carmela Soprano on HBO's *The Sopranos*,
actress Edie Falco earned an Emmy, Golden Globe, and
Screen Actors Guild Award for her portrayal of the mafia
wife. Her credits also include appearances on HBO's *Oz*,
and the films *Unbelievable Truth* (1989), *Trust* (1991),
Judy Berlin (2000), and *Random Hearts* (2000). Recently
she returned to the stage, starring in Broadway's *Frankie
and Johnny in the Clair de Lune*.

FIONNULA FLANAGAN

Award-winning actress Fionnula Flanagan has starred on
stage and in films. Her credits include the theatrical pro-
ductions *Ulysses in Nighttown* and *James Joyce's Women*
(1977), for which she won Critics Circle Awards in Los
Angeles and San Francisco. Flanagan also received an
Emmy for her work in the television miniseries *Rich Man,
Poor Man*. She most recently appeared in the films
Divine Secrets of the Ya-Ya Sisterhood (2002), *The Others*
(2001), *With or Without You* (1999), and *Waking Ned
Devine* (1998).

TERI GARR

Actress Teri Garr began her career as a dancer in the
Elvis Presley films *Fun in Acapulco* (1963) and *Viva Las
Vegas* (1964). Her acting career led her to comedic roles
in the films *Young Frankenstein* (1974), *Oh, God!* (1977),
and *Mr. Mom* (1983). Garr's portrayal of Dustin Hoffman's
girlfriend in the hit comedy *Tootsie* (1981) earned her an
Academy Award nomination. Garr has guest-starred on
television programs such as *Friends* and *Felicity*.

SUE GRAFTON

International bestselling author Sue Grafton began the popular mystery series featuring private detective Kinsey Millhone in 1982 with *A Is for Alibi* (1982). She has since made her way through the alphabet, with titles such as *C Is for Corpse* (1986), *M Is for Malice* (1996), *P Is for Peril* (2001), and the latest, *Q Is for Quarry* (2003).

DENYCE GRAVES

Mezzo-soprano Denyce Graves made her debut at the Metropolitan Opera in the title role of *Carmen* in the 1995–96 season. A noted recitalist with a broad repertoire, she has released over a dozen CDs and performed at opera houses all over the world. She recently appeared in a new production of *Samson et Dalila*, opposite Placido Domingo, at the Metropolitan Opera.

MELANIE GRIFFITH

Melanie Griffith's film credits include *Night Moves* (1975), *Body Double* (1984), *Something Wild* (1986), and *The Milagro Beanfield War* (1988). She is perhaps most famous for playing Tess McGill in *Working Girl* (1988), a role that won her an Academy Award nomination. She will hit Broadway in 2003 as Roxy Hart in the musical, *Chicago*.

CHERRY JONES

Cherry Jones, a founding member of the American
Repertory Theatre in Cambridge, Massachusetts, spent
much of her early career acting on stage. She has starred
in such Broadway productions as *Angels in America*, *The
Night of the Iguana*, *Our Country's Good*, and *A Moon for
the Misbegotten*. Her performance in the 1995 produc-
tion of *The Heiress* earned her the prestigious Tony
Award. Jones has also appeared in the films *A League of
Their Own* (1992), *The Horse Whisperer* (1998), *Erin
Brockovich* (2000), *The Perfect Storm* (2000), and *Divine
Secrets of the Ya-Ya Sisterhood* (2002).

JANE KACZMAREK

Actress Jane Kaczmarek has appeared on stage and in film.
She currently stars in Fox television's *Malcolm in the Middle*
as the mother of four children. Her feature film credits
include *Pleasantville* and *The Chamber*, and she also
appeared on Broadway in Neil Simon's *Lost in Yonkers*.

ALEX KINGSTON

Best known as Dr. Elizabeth Corday on the television series
ER, Alex Kingston spent much of her early career onstage
as a member of England's Royal Shakespeare Company.
Her feature-film credits include *Croupier* (1998),
Carrington (1995), and *The Cook, The Thief, His Wife and
Her Lover* (1989).

GLADYS KNIGHT

Gladys Knight was eight years old when, along with family members, she formed the group the Pips, later known as Gladys Knight and the Pips. Their first hit was "I Heard It Through the Grapevine" (1967) and they won their first Grammy for "Neither One of Us Wants to Be the First to Say Goodbye" in 1973. The group went on to amass a series of gold records and Grammy awards and was inducted into the Rock and Roll Hall of Fame in 1996. Gladys Knight published her autobiography, *Between Each Line of Pain and Glory: My Life Story*, in 1997.

LISA LESLIE

Lisa Leslie, the Los Angeles Sparks center, became the first player in the history of the WNBA to win the regular season MVP, the All-Star Game MVP, and the play-off MVP in the same season. She is the recipient of two Olympic gold medals in basketball, and in June 2002 she became the first woman in the professional league to do a one-handed slam dunk in a game.

LISA LING

Lisa Ling began her television career at age sixteen as one of the hosts of *Scratch*, a Sacramento-based nationally syndicated teen magazine show. She continued her career at Channel One, a network broadcast in schools across the country, and eventually became a senior war corre-spondent at the network. In 1999 she joined the cast of ABC's *The View* and in 2003 left the talk show to become the host of MSNBC's *National Geographic Explorer*.

SUSAN LUCCI

Best known as Erica Kane on the daytime soap opera *All My Children*, Susan Lucci has portrayed the villainess since 1970. She was nominated for eighteen daytime Emmy awards as Outstanding Lead Actress in a Drama Series and finally took home the statue in an emotional 1999 telecast. In addition to her Emmy, she is the recipient of an American Academy of Achievement Award, a People's Choice Award, and a Soap Opera Digest Award. She has starred in many made-for-television movies, and played Annie Oakley in the Broadway musical *Annie Get Your Gun*.

WENDIE MALICK

Actress Wendie Malick has starred in two long-running comedy series, HBO's *Dream On* and NBC's *Just Shoot Me*, and has received two Emmy nominations for her work. She has also appeared in numerous films and movies for television, and was the voice of ChiCha in Disney's animated feature *The Emperor's New Groove* (2001).

JO DEE MESSINA

A multiplatinum country singer, Jo Dee Messina has received the Country Music Association's prestigious Horizon Award recognizing career growth, the Academy of Country Music's Top New Female Vocalist Award, and the Boston Music Awards' Artist of the Year. Her last new album was *Burn*, and her *Greatest Hits* album was released in spring 2003.

RITA MORENO

Best known for her Academy Award-winning performance in the musical *West Side Story* (1961), Rita Moreno has a distinguished list of film credits to her name: *Singin' in the Rain* (1952), *The King and I* (1956), *Carnal Knowledge* (1971), *The Four Seasons* (1981), and *The Slums of Beverly Hills* (1998). In 1975 Moreno won a Tony Award for her performance in *The Ritz*, a role she reprised for the film adaptation. Moreno spent five years as a member of the ensemble cast of the children's show *The Electric Company* and has also won Emmys for guest appearances on *The Muppet Show* (1977) and *The Rockford Files* (1978). From 1997 until 2003, Moreno starred in the HBO series *Oz*, winning three ALMA awards for her portrayal of Sister Marie.

DEE DEE MYERS

White House Press Secretary under President Clinton from 1993 until 1994, Dee Dee Myers has since been a cohost on NBC's *Equal Time*, a political analyst, lecturer, and a consultant to NBC's *The West Wing*.

KATHY NAJIMY

Actress Kathy Najimy began her career in an Obie Award-winning off-Broadway show she cowrote entitled *The Kathy and Mo Show*. To her credit the show was adapted for television by HBO and garnered Najimy several Cable ACE awards. She has performed both in film and television, currently providing the voice for Peggy Hill on Fox's animated comedy *King of the Hill*. Kathy is also well known for her activism and was the 2002 recipient of PETA's Humanitarian of the Year Award.

CYNTHIA NIXON

Cynthia Nixon made her film debut at the age of fourteen in the film *Little Darlings* (1980), and went on to appear in *Prince of the City* (1981), *Amadeus* (1984), and *Addams Family Values* (1993). Cynthia is a founding member of the Drama Dept, a New York–based theater company, and a recipient of a Theater World Award and a Los Angeles Drama Critics Award. Her stage credits include *The Heidi Chronicles*, *Who's Afraid of Virginia Woolf?*, and *The Philadelphia Story*. Currently she costars in the groundbreaking HBO series *Sex and the City*.

ELIZABETH PERKINS

Elizabeth Perkins made her theatrical debut in *Brighton Beach Memoirs* and has appeared in numerous films including *About Last Night* (1986), *Big* (1988), *The Doctor* (1991), and *The Flintstones* (1996). She has also starred in the NBC television series *Battery Park*, and HBO's *If These Walls Could Talk*.

JANE PRATT

In addition to being Editor in Chief of *JANE* magazine, Jane Pratt is the author of two books, *For Real: The Uncensored Truth About America's Teenagers* and *Beyond Beauty: Girls Speak Out on Looks, Style, and Stereotypes*. No stranger to the publishing and entertainment business, she was the founding editor of *SASSY* magazine and hosted two talk shows.

KELLY PRESTON

Kelly Preston found her first success in mainstream feature films in *Twins* (1988) and has since had roles in the films *From Dusk Till Dawn* (1996), *Jerry Maguire* (1996), and *Battlefield Earth: A Saga of the Year 3000* (2000). Recent film credits include *What a Girl Wants* (2003) and *The Cat in the Hat* (2003).

ANNA QUINDLEN

Anna Quindlen was a columnist for the op-ed page for the *New York Times* and a collection of her columns, *Thinking Out Loud*, was a national bestseller and Pulitzer Prize winner. In 1995 she became a novelist and has written *Object Lessons*, *One True Thing*, *Black and Blue*, *Blessed*, and the best-seller *A Short Guide to a Happy Life*. She currently writes a biweekly column in *Newsweek*.

SALLY RIDE

Astronaut and astrophysicist, Sally Ride was awarded a position in NASA's astronaut program in 1978 and in 1983 joined the crew of the space shuttle *Challenger*. She served on a presidential commission investigating the space shuttle *Challenger* accident (1986), and as Special Assistant to the Administrator, NASA (1987).

MICHELLE RODRIGUEZ

Michelle Rodriguez first gained major recognition for her role as a young female boxer in the independent film *Girlfight* (2000). The role earned her the Deauville Festival of American Cinema Award for Best Actress and the Las Vegas Film Critics Society Award for Female Breakthrough Performance. She has since appeared in the films *The Fast and the Furious* (2001) and *Blue Crush* (2002).

AMY SEDARIS

Amy Sedaris conceived and starred in Comedy Central's television series *Strangers with Candy*. As half of *The Talent Family*, she has collaborated with her brother on many off-Broadway plays, including *One Woman Shoe*, for which they were awarded an Obie, and *The Book of Liz*. She costarred in the sketch comedy series *Exit 57*, and has appeared on *Sex and the City*. She also recently appeared in the film *Maid in Manhattan* (2002).

JAMIE-LYNN SIGLER

Jamie-Lynn Sigler, an actress and singer, is best known for her role as Meadow Soprano on HBO's original series *The Sopranos*. In 2002 she was cast as the lead in Disney's Broadway production of *Beauty and the Beast* and in 2003 had her autobiography, *Wise Girl*, published.

JEAN SMART

Jean Smart's career first began in the theater; she appeared on Broadway in *Piaf* and in the off-Broadway play *Last Summer at Bluefish Cove*. In 1986 Smart joined the cast of the television series *Designing Women* and remained on the show for five seasons. Her feature films include *The Brady Bunch Movie* (1995), *Sweet Home Alabama* (2002), and *Bringing Down the House* (2003). Most recently she guest-starred on *Frasier* and won two Emmy awards for her performance on the sitcom.

MARY STEENBURGEN

Actress Mary Steenburgen made her film debut in *Goin' South* (1978), and two years later won a Best Supporting Actress Oscar for her performance in *Melvin and Howard* (1980). She has appeared in the films *Ragtime* (1981), *Parenthood* (1989), *Philadelphia* (1993), and starred in the made-for-TV series *Gulliver's Travels* (1996) and *Living with the Dead* (2002).

TANYA TUCKER

Tanya Tucker is known for bringing rock and roll style to country music. With over thirty albums to her credit, including *Best of My Love*, *Complicated*, and *Tanya*, she has won numerous awards, including the Country Music Association's Female Vocalist of the Year and the Academy of Country Music's Video of the Year. In 1993 she was inducted into the Country Music Hall of Fame's Walkway of Stars.

LEE ANN WOMACK

Lee Ann Womack's music has been described as country music for lovers. Her 1997 debut album garnered her instant success with the platinum number-one single "The Fool." In 2000 the title song of her album *I Hope You Dance* won the Country Music Association's awards for Single of the Year and Song of the Year, and in 2001 Lee Ann won the CMA for Female Vocalist of the Year.

when i was a girl . . .

denyce graves

I thought I would grow up to be many different things: a nun, a nurse, an actress . . . and now I realize that who I am today is the person that I am becoming.

kelly preston

I was chubby, I was a moppet.
I was really happy, very
secure, knowing I could do
whatever I wanted. I was very
available and so loved.

sue grafton

I had little ringlets that my mother
would do in what she called a rattail
comb. I was what they call one of
life's little cheerleaders. I discovered
if you do a little tap dance, you can
get away with murder.

The Fifties

I WORE

Black velvet ribbon chokers
Felt poodle skirts
Angora sweaters
Homemade headbands
Charm bracelets
Keds
Sweater sets
Pearls
A boyfriend's ring on a
    chain
Scuffed suede shoes
A pageboy haircut
Shoelaces with bells
Horsehair crinolines
Bangs
Pastel Capezio flats
Cinch belts
Penny loafers
Neckerchiefs
Peter Pan collars

I ATE/DRANK

Tuna melts
Skippy peanut butter
Welch's grape jelly
Cherry Kool-Aid powder
    out of my hand
Turkish Taffy
Malteds
Frappes
Vanilla Cokes
Lime rickeys
Cherry sundaes
Good Humor bars

I DANCED

The Miami Beach Rumba
The Stroll
The Hand Jive
The Shim Sham
The Bunny Hop
The Hokey Pokey
Ball and the Jack

I WORSHIPED

Grace Kelly
Eddie Fisher
Marilyn Monroe
Gene Kelly
Elvis
James Dean
Natalie Wood

I WATCHED

The Ed Sullivan Show
The Kate Smith Hour
Molly Goldberg
I Remember Mama
Sky King
Howdy Doody
Milton Berle Show
American Bandstand
The $64,000 Question
Hit Parade
Your Show of Shows
Name That Tune
Beat the Clock
What's My Line

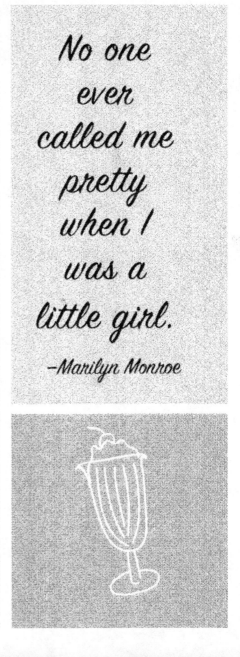

No one ever called me pretty when I was a little girl.

—Marilyn Monroe

I LISTENED TO

Gene Shepard on the
   radio
Fibber McGee and Molly
   on the radio
Elvis Presley
Paul Anka
Johnnie Mathis
Frank Sinatra
Rosemary Clooney
Harry Belafonte
Chubby Checker

I READ

The Bobbsey Twins
Seventeen magazine
Peyton Place by Grace
   Metalious
The Blackboard Jungle by
   Evan Hunter
Little Women by Louisa
   May Alcott
American Girl magazine

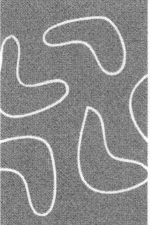

I USED

Bonne Bell lipstick in tangerine

White lipstick

Helena Rubenstein's Beauty Grains

Cherries in the Snow lipstick by
    Revlon

Lily of the Valley perfume

Yardley Super Pink lipstick

The Fifties

lisa ling

I grew up outside of Sacramento, California, in a town called Carmichael. My parents got a divorce when I was seven. My father and mother were just extremely different people who probably should never have been married in the first place. The divorce was extremely difficult, though in hindsight it was probably the best thing that could have happened to my sister and me. It allowed us to be exposed to entirely different kinds of lifestyles and to entirely different kinds of people.

My father was extremely strict. He was a small Chinese man with a really loud voice and he ruled by fear. He was so strict, he literally had to point to a chopstick on the wall when I did something wrong and it would stop me from doing it. I'd get spanked with a chopstick. It certainly wasn't an abusive kind of spanking, but it was just like a tap—a reminder that what I was doing wasn't right.

I'd get spanked with a chopstick. It certainly wasn't an abusive kind of spanking, but it was just like a tap— a reminder that what I was doing wasn't right.

My sister was—and is—my best friend in the world. She knows me better than I know myself. Because of the divorce, my relationship with my parents was a little volatile. That made me become very maternal toward her. I called her my little baby. To this day, she complains "I'm not a little baby. I'm twenty-five years old." But we were very, very close and I always felt that nurturing responsibility toward her. In fact, I cried when I found out she'd been with a man. It was devastating to me. But I've matured and she's matured. I've always had a more overt personality, been the one on TV; but she's so much smarter than I could ever possibly be, and so much more stable. For someone who's three years younger than me, she has just been a very wise authoritative voice in my life. She's my backbone.

After the divorce, my mom moved to Los Angeles. She would come back every month and I would talk to her on the phone every day. My dad worked, so my sister and I basically came home and watched TV all day long. The TV was our babysitter. Our grandmother, my father's mother, was there quite a bit too; she would force us to have Bible study every day, so our house was the house that kids wanted to stay away from. They knew that once they got close, they'd be corralled into having Bible study. It was extremely embarrassing and frustrating.

> She would force us to have Bible study every day, so our house was the house that kids wanted to stay away from.

My grandmother was really the one who raised us. She enjoyed going on long car rides, so every weekend my father would load my sister and me in the back of the car and we'd go for what my grandmother called "a *rounding*." She was raised in England, so she had a little bit of a British accent, so she'd say: "Let's go for a round-ing." My sister and I hated roundings; they were so monotonous and boring. We'd sit in the backseat with our Walkmans on listen-ing to Duran Duran and Quiet Riot at the top volume level. We'd go from Sacramento

to San Francisco—about a two-hour drive—
and have dim sum. You know, as a kid all
you want is pizza. But it was really the one
thing that made my grandmother happy—
being able to go on these trips and have
her dim sum on weekends.

Holidays for us. Well, every Fourth
of July we'd sit on our land and my father
would buy us sparklers. My sister and I
were obsessed with fire and matches; we'd
carry these sparklers and twist them
around and watch the fireworks. It was
great. My father made the best marinated
barbecue chicken, and he'd always break it
out Fourth of July. To this day, he hasn't
revealed his secret and I think that's
because he doesn't even know what's in the
recipe—he just puts whatever happens to
be on the shelf in, and somehow it comes
out delicious.

I hated Thanksgiving, growing up,
because all of my friends at Switzer
Elementary School came back with stories
about turkey and stuffing, cranberries and
sweet potatoes, and we never had that
experience. We always went to Chinese
restaurants for Thanksgiving and had
Peking duck. A Chinese restaurant will
always be open on Thanksgiving, because
that's what Chinese people do.

As for Christmas, I always believed

Santa Claus didn't like Chinese kids. They don't celebrate Christmas in China. My dad always made attempts to get trees; they were always these little skinny trees that he could carry by himself. Unfortunately, his idea of gifts from Santa were boxes of Goldfish crackers and twenty dollars. All the other kids were getting bikes and stereos and TVs. It's funny. I was dating this Korean guy, and he had a similar experience, except he didn't even get a tree. So maybe Santa Claus really doesn't like Asian kids. Maybe that's true! Hey, Santa, start giving the Asian kids some love!

Hey, Santa, start giving the Asian kids some love!

If I could have one wish it would be to have one more day with my grandmother—just one more day. I was sixteen years old when I started working in TV. I was on a show called *Scratch*. It was a nationally syndicated magazine show. She was just starting to get senile at this time. We'd be sitting in the living room, *Scratch* would come on, and she'd look at the TV, then look at me, then look at the TV and exclaim, "Lisa, that girl looks just like you!"

LISA LING

I'd say, "Grandmother, that *is* me!"

"NO!" she'd shout.

This happened every single Saturday.

My family wasn't overtly affection-ate. They'd be embarrassed when I would wrap my arms around them and be cozy with them. Exhibiting so much affection wasn't part of their culture. My grandmother would come up to me and sniff my cheek. That was how she was affectionate. I find myself doing that with little kids now too—it's the weirdest thing. It was those little things—when she sniffed me or my dad kissed me on the cheek when I was sleeping—that have become so dear to me.

I loved those moments. Looking out the window with her little hand on mine.

When my grandmother became senile, she barely remembered anything except my sister and me. The nurse at the convalescent home told me she used to scream our names: "Lisa, Laura, where are you?" Sometimes I'd pick her up from the home and take her on a drive. I drove a stick-shift car, and I remember being in the middle of driving and suddenly feeling this bony little hand on top of my own.

I loved those moments. Looking out the window with her little hand on mine. I just wish that I could have that again.

home

&

family

Be a **first-rate version** of **yourself**, not a second-rate version of **someone else.**

—Judy Garland

my bedroom

candice **bergen**

In my bedroom, I had twin beds, a collection of horses, and a little plastic crucifix that glowed in the dark—it was the glowing rather than the religion aspect that attracted me. I had what was then called a Victrola, a Walt Disney's *Snow White* record player that played only 45s. There were morning glories growing out the window and lots of dogs—real dogs, that is.

alex kingston

It was a wonderful child's room. We had a bunk bed. My sister was on the bottom, I was on the top. We had a rocking horse, and I'd rock on that horse like crazy. The walls were completely covered with toys. My father made a little walk-in cupboard where I could sit in a tiny rocking chair, read books, and feel like I was in my own secret place. It was very nice for me, growing up.

cherry jones

When I was really tiny, I shared a little garret room with my parents. There were morning doves cooing outside the window. Apparently, as a nine-month-old, I did a wicked imitation of a dove. Once we moved, I had this amazing room that was sort of like the inside of a chest. It had red wallpaper and old furniture. My family had been pioneer Tennessee people, so they had all this wonderful furniture from the nineteenth century that had been acquired over 150 years.

I had, on the wall, an old photo that belonged to my great-great-grandfather Stevens; also a fiddle that was all worn down from where his fingers had played it for years. Inside the violin, there was a rattlesnake. I guess they did it for luck, put rattlesnakes in fiddles. We would always shake the violin and listen to those rattles. Eventually, I managed to get them out. I was sorry about that.

teri garr

We lived in this house in the Valley and we had to rent out the front of it because we couldn't afford it. My father had stopped working; my mother wasn't working, so we all lived in one room in the back. My brothers and I had bunk beds. The big thing, of course, was who got to be on the top bunk bed. No matter what happened—atomic bomb, who cares—all that mattered was the top bunk. That was the most important thing.

In that house, when we lived in the back room, everyone ate in shifts. A lot of my father's friends who came from vaudeville would visit us and eat dinner at the table, so there were all these crazy show business people from all over the world eating in our bedroom, and we'd hear stories about vaudeville or the Folies Bergeres.

anna quindlen

My bed had a dust ruffle. I don't know how a mother can put a dust ruffle on her child's bed. I mean, I understand the design aspect of it. But the terror aspect of it? It's huge. I used to run from the door of my room, then spring up and land on my bed. I'd get high enough, so that whatever was going to come up from under the dust ruffle wouldn't get me.

ellen burstyn

I had a wonderful bedroom. I adored my bedroom. It was actually a sunroom, and it had no heating. We lived in Detroit, and my mom always felt really guilty about putting us in that cold room. But I loved it. There were windows on all sides. I could open the window and the trees would come inside the room, and I just loved that. It was a small room with a yellow bedspread with blue trim. I had white furniture and dolls on my bed.

illeana douglas

My bedroom went through many phases. The worst phase, probably, was when I decided to paint everything. We lived in a colonial house. My father said it was important that I express myself creatively, and so I painted my room lime green and purple, which later took about eighty coats of paint to get off. Then I went into my art deco phase; there was silver wallpaper and everything was black. That was really bad too. Finally, I did something with three shades of blue. It was a really, really small room; actually, it wasn't a room, it was more like a corridor. I made collages of movie stars' faces. I had Al Pacino and Richard Dreyfuss and Marlon Brando. There were all these famous faces looking at me.

fionnula flanagan

My girlhood bedroom was very crowded, because I had two sisters and I grew up in a place where, unless you were extremely wealthy, the concept of having your own room as a child just didn't exist. I shared a room with my brother until we were four or five and then with my two sisters after that. When I was about sixteen I still didn't have a room to myself. There were a lot of boxes that had *Don't touch that! That's mine!* written on them. My sisters were younger than I, so they were always stealing my clothes and trying on my shoes. Their dolls would be scattered all over the place. It was a very untidy room, too small for three people, but my memory of it is that it was bigger than it was.

ann curry

When I close my eyes and think about my childhood bedroom, I think of so many bedrooms because we moved around so often. The one thing that comes to mind is this cream-colored corduroy bedspread with pinkish roses and green leaves, and it was so soft and cozy and I just felt good lying on my bed on top of it. It was a kind of permanent thing in my ever-changing world, because when you are a military brat, the thing you get really used to is change.

jamie-lynn sigler

My room was everything pink. Everything from my tool chest to my sheets to my clothes, everything. I had twenty-five to thirty porcelain dolls surrounding my bedroom set. I had tons of pillows and stuffed animals. It was a comforting room—I think the color pink is comforting to me.

lisa leslie

I was wide-eyed and quiet. I didn't talk a whole lot, but I loved being around my mom and listening to her. I was very much a crybaby—especially where my mom was concerned.

When I was little, my mother was a mail carrier. She'd get up at 5:30 A.M. Every morning I'd go in her room and help pick out her shoes and just try and assist her in getting dressed—as if she needed help. Then I'd walk her to the door, she'd leave, and I'd get in her bed, look through her photo album at pictures of her and cry. I'd cry and cry, then fall back to sleep.

My sister would wake me up a couple hours later and she'd tell me, "Something's wrong with you. You are crazy." I probably did that for five years. It was a little odd, but I really loved my mom and I hated the fact that she had to leave and go to work.

My father was gone. I actually didn't see my father until I was twelve years old. I believe my mom said he lived with us for a little bit when I was two months old. But he left again, so I feel like I didn't know him.

Did I miss not having two parents in my household? I think when you are a kid, you don't know what you're missing if you never had it. I don't remember inquiring about my father. I had all this love for my mom. I just wanted to go and do whatever she did. She was the mother and the father in my family. I don't remember having issues with kids at school or *knowing* that I didn't know my father. I don't remember talking about him or feeling like I needed to find him or know exactly where he was.

She was the mother and the father in my family.

My mom was very feminine. She always had her nails done and polished and her hair was always very neat, very clean. At the same time, my mother was very strong. We mowed the lawn in the front- and backyards; we raked the leaves; we mopped and waxed. We did everything a man would have done around the house as well as what a woman would do, whether it was indoors or outdoors.

She was very loving, but also very strict. There were rules. Like how we couldn't say the word *butt*. Or we had to be inside the house before the streetlights came on. If you saw them flicker, you better be on your way into the house. I remember one day I was outside jumping rope and the streetlights came on, and I continued to jump rope, and before I knew it my mother was standing there on the porch with her hands on her hips, giving me a look. She didn't have to say a lot. That look was enough. I took my ropes, threw them in the backyard, ran to the front door and my mom was standing there.

I got hit. I tried to dive past it, past her hand, but I didn't quite make it. My mom hitting me was enough to put the fear in me to get in the house before the streetlights came on.

My mom became a truck driver. She drove an 18-wheeler across the country and would be gone for a whole month at a time. It was a big disappointment, not having her there always. I was so attached to her. She called me "the shadow." Everywhere she went, I went. I was eleven at this point. I had a little sister now.

"Remember girls, books before boys"

We were moved around from my aunt's house to my grandmother's house. Sometimes we had housekeepers. We had to adjust to so many different people. It was very uncomfortable sometimes. I always felt like I was walking on eggshells. I felt I had to protect not only myself but my little sister, who was three. So if she dropped something or spilled something, I'd be very nervous.

My mom being away allowed for other people to impact my life. I had my Aunt Judy, who always gave us positive affirmations. She'd tell me I was going to be a writer, that I was very observant. There was my Aunt Bernice. She'd always say, "Remember girls, books before boys, books

before boys." And there was my grandmother, who was a nurse. She'd gone to
college and she was very proud of that.

I remember times when my cousins
would ask me if I felt poor. I'd always think, *I
don't feel poor.* Even if we went to the swap
meet, to me it was what we could do and it
was fine. I was appreciative of what my
mom was able to provide.

I actually was in the truck with my
mom one summer. I was twelve. We had
flown to Dallas, and were heading to
Baltimore, which is where my father was
from. I guess somehow my mom got in
touch with his family. She called them, and
he was there and wanted to come over to
the hotel to meet me. I remember being
outside swimming. I was just burned up,
and my hair was a mess. My mom said,
"Lisa, come get out of the pool. Your
father's going to come over. Get dressed."

I was nervous. I didn't know what I'd
say to him, what I'd call him.

I got dressed, and he knocked on
the door, and it was just one of those
things. He was really handsome, frowning,
with nice curly hair. I was looking at him,
and I could see myself a little bit—and my
older sister too. I said, "I don't know what I
should call you." He said, "Well, you can call

me whatever you want." But I didn't call him anything. And that was the last time I saw him. He passed away in 1985 of stomach cancer.

Every month, my mom would come home for three days. To hear my mother's truck coming around that corner, knowing that she was coming home—that was the happiest time. We'd come out of the house screaming and cheering. You'd think that Santa Claus was there. That was the best feeling, my mom being home. We always knew that it was for a short period of time, but those were always the happiest days. We'd just take off her shoes and rub her feet and get the shower ready. We wanted to make her feel comfortable, because we knew within two days she had to be back out on the road.

family

edie falco

When I was a girl, I thought my mother was God. That's the truth. I thought she was the funniest, most creative, most beautiful, most talented, and definitely the coolest—although cool meant a different thing at the time. And she was just breathtaking. I remember being quite certain that she was the most beautiful person in the world. She had huge blue eyes, red, red long hair, which she wore with little bangs and a headband. She had these high cheekbones and a very expressive face.

My mother was an amazing, powerful woman. She was just all there was.

> # I was brought up by two extremely intelligent people who gave me the greatest gift . . . freedom from fear.
>
> **—Katharine Hepburn**

I never quite knew what she did for her job. All I knew was that she'd get up in the morning; I'd hear 1010 WINS in her room; she'd be putting on her makeup; I'd smell her perfume. She'd emerge, done up, in a skirt, high heels clicking, get into her car, and drive off to her job. At the time, not many moms were working. I just thought that was so cool.

ellen degeneres

My brother used to pay me to stay away from him. He'd give me a nickel. I'm sure kids get paid a lot more now, but at the time, in the '60s, I got a nickel or a dime to just stay away from him and his friends. I was three years younger and they didn't want to have anything to do with me.

jane kaczmarek

My father was a very domineering figure. He worked for the Defense Department and he was in the air force reserve, so he was always on an air force base. We would visit him and everyone would always salute him, which my mother found hysterically funny. I grew up thinking my father knew everything, that he was the best of everything. But he was quite a disciplinarian and a scary figure. I had two brothers and one sister. We were very close—I think the children get very close when you have an adversary in the house—in our case, a dad coming home and often not being pleased with what he found there.

We were given traditional roles: Boys had to do yard work, girls had to do housework, which never seemed fair because that meant doing dishes every day and they had to shovel snow once a week, one season a year. We were the house slaves and they were the yard slaves.

We were the house slaves and they were the yard slaves.

We couldn't have Beatles albums, we couldn't have Monkeys albums, we couldn't listen to rock and roll. As my father said, it was a Communist plot. To this day, I've never heard my parents say d-a-m-n. I remember coming home from college and my brother using some expletive. My father took him into the other room and reprimanded him. "Billy, please choose another word with which to express yourself. The English language is a beautiful language and we don't use those words in this house." It's amazing to think that in this day and age, there are still people like my parents walking around, saying things like "I was so mad, I thought I'd have kittens."

chris evert

My mom was almost too good to be true. I never heard her say a bad word about anybody. At matches, she would always clap for both me and my opponent. She'd go up to the player after the match. If the player won, my mom would congratulate her. If I won, my mom would console her. "Don't worry," my mom would say. "You'll get her next time." By her, she meant me. I said, "Mom, I think that's going a bit too far." Telling my opponent she'll get me next time? That's stepping over the line.

joan chen

There was a time when both of my parents were sent away, and so my brother and I were sort of on our own as little children. We were given a box of candies each as a comfort and I would suck on candy before bed. And, of course, I got all these cavities. So when I was a girl, I hated going to the dentist. And I had to go a lot.

melanie griffith

My parents got divorced when I was three. Alfred
Hitchcock saw my mother, Tippy Hedren, in a soap
commercial and brought her out to Hollywood. So I
grew up going back and forth all the time. I'd go from
my dad in New York to my mom in Los Angeles, and
all I wanted was to live in Kansas so that they could
be the ones who'd come and visit me. And that way, I
could wear ruby red slippers too.

My mother and stepfather went to Africa in
1972 and found themselves stricken by the plight of
animals there. There was a prediction that by the
year 2000 there would be no more wild animals.
My stepfather made a movie about it, and my mother
decided that we should get a real lion—that way, we
could experience what living with wildlife was like. So
we made friends with this guy Neil. He had a full-
grown lion on his ranch, and we'd go out and visit
him. Eventually, we got a lion cub of our own. His
name was Casey, and he was our first cat. Eventually,
we started to get more and more. The police would
come to our door, and I'd take the lions, jump over
the fence into this vacant lot, and hide there with the
cats while the police searched the house. It was a
wild thing to do.

If I could go back to a place from my childhood, it would be to my father's place in New York. It
was called Hanker's Farm. He had 350 acres of
wilderness—it's East Coast wilderness, which is so different from California. There's something so special
about the light. There was all this corn planted there.
I remember running free in the fields and stealing
ears of corn. There was just all this land to get lost in.

rita moreno

I thought of my father as very handsome, a slick kind of guy. He had a lot of ladies on the side, which is why my mother ended up getting a divorce and leaving Puerto Rico. He was short with this thin little gigolo kind of mustache, and his hair was very slicked back with pomade.

You didn't do things with your daughter unless you were an unusual man.

I don't have specific memories of him, because we didn't do things together. But that was typical: Where I grew up, in this little town in Puerto Rico, you didn't do things with your daughter unless you were an unusual man. If you had a son, you did things with him, but you didn't do things with your daughter. I doubt that he knew what I was about or what I did, who my little kid friends were, or where I spent my hours when I wasn't home. I don't think he knew a thing about me. So very early in life, I began to think that men were not terrific with girls. And I got a very fixed idea of what Latino men were like.

After her divorce from my father, my mother left me with him for a period of time and took a ship to New York City—as many Puerto Rican women at the time did—to make some money. She very young, she was about nineteen, she was a baby. And she stayed with an aunt in the Hispanic ghetto and got a job in a sweatshop as a seamstress along with who knows how many thousands of other Hispanic women. When she'd made enough money, and learned enough English, she went back to Puerto Rico to retrieve me. That was probably six months later. I remember seeing her come back and not being that familiar with her. I knew her, but somehow she seemed odd to me. She brought a trunk with her, and in the trunk were toys. They were there for a very specific reason: to entice me to come back with her.

sandra bernhard

My mother is an abstract artist, a Libra, and left-handed. She is a really smart, creative person. It's not like she's a freak—she's just unusual in her own way, outspoken in a very soft-spoken manner. She has no filters. She'll just say things that are totally out there. They're more funny than embarrassing. Though one time, my mom *did* really embarrass me. Somebody called my house, pretending they were me all doped up. I was at the movies at the time, seeing *The Odd Couple*. Anyway, my mom freaked out and came running into the movie theater. She was in lime green stretch pants and she was calling out my name. My mother would totally cross the line.

kathy najimy

My memory of my dad? He was either going to work, coming home from work, or sleeping. He worked two jobs: He was a butcher at the grocery store during the day, and he worked at the post office at night. The time we *did* spend with him could be very intense: either crazy, wild impromptu, spur-of-the-moment great-big-surprise fun or the exact opposite. My dad could be very volatile. He had a very bad temper. It could get very scary. Things would be thrown everywhere.

My dad was famous for inviting the kids in the class to come and have these great wild games. I remember once he hung this string from the ceiling. He attached jelly doughnuts to the string and we had to get on our knees, with our hands tied behind our backs, and try to eat the jelly doughnuts. It was always hilarious. This other time, he took a poll of the party by asking, "Who is the bravest one here?" This little boy named Reuben raised his hand.

Well, my dad had strewn broken glass all over newspapers in the living room. He told Reuben, "We're going to blindfold you and take off your shoes and have you walk through the glass." While Reuben was getting his blindfold on, we removed the glass and put cooked spaghetti down on the floor. I don't know how my dad came up with these ideas. But either he was playing crazy games or about to lose his temper and hide in the bedroom. That was the tone in our household. It wasn't the healthiest, but it wasn't the worst either.

jamie-lynn sigler

My mother was the coolest lady around. To me, she had superpowers. If I had a stomachache, if I had a headache, I honestly believed that if my mom rubbed my head, the ache would go away. I still get like that too. She is the first person I turn to whenever I have a major dilemma. She has the same relationship with her mom, so the three of us have always done stuff together.

My brothers called me "Small Fry" and "Lemonade." I don't know where *lemonade* came from. I was always in the middle and they loved to torture me, because I was so gullible. I wanted to play with them, and would let them do anything to me. I would let them dress me up in goalie equipment and take shots at me in front of a hockey goal—just so I could hang out with them.

gillian anderson

When I think of my mother, I think of her walking me to nursery school. We had a running argument about how much she loved me versus how much I loved her. It was very important that I loved her more than she loved me.

cherry jones

I lived with my great-grandmother, Mama; my grandmother, Thelma Cherry; and my mother and my
father. There were four generations of women in the
same little house. There was also a woman who
helped rear me. Her name was Odessa Mitchum, and
we had an incredibly close bond. She would let me
run wild by day, and then my parents would come
home at night and the discipline would begin.

My mother was an English teacher, my father
had a flower shop, and my grandmother worked at
the flower shop. My parents looked liked movie stars.
Everyone says so. They were this beautiful young
couple in town, and they were the pillars of the
Methodist church. They both had beautiful singing
voices. They had an unusual
sense of style and a real
sense of dignity. They
were very compassion-
ate people. It was just
such a pleasure and
privilege to grow up
their child.

elizabeth **perkins**

When I was a girl, I thought my mother was very lonely. My father left and she was ill-equipped to go out into the world and work. She came from the generation where you went to a fine women's college, you got married in your third year, and then you became a housewife and mother. She had no preparation, and suddenly she was out there on her own. She'd never worked a day in her life, she never supported herself. This was 1966 or 1967 and there was no real groundwork or support system to help her make this huge transition. She was very lonely and very sad for a lot of those years, and I remember late nights with my sister, listening at the door while my mother cried in the bedroom.

My mother got into a pretty abusive relationship. I was about eleven and living in the middle of nowhere. We were maybe three miles from the nearest house and I remember thinking *It's either sink or swim.* I got up in the middle of the night, I packed my bags, and I walked and I walked and I walked and I walked. I had thirty dollars in my pocket, I got on a Greyhound bus, and I took it to go see my sister, who was—at this point—in school away from home.

I got up in the middle
of the night,
I packed my bags,
and I walked
and I walked
and I walked
and I walked.

I look back on that now, and I see my daughter who's eleven, and wonder how I felt strong enough to do that. I didn't care that I was walking down a deserted road at two o'clock in the morning with thirty dollars in my pocket, that I had to get on a bus by myself. It was very powerful for me. It made me feel like I could do anything.

holidays

melanie griffith

I took Valentine's Day very seriously. I had a canopy bed, and Valentine's Day I'd wake up to find hearts hanging everywhere. My mother would do sweet things like that.

> **I stopped believing in** Santa Claus when I was six. Mother took me to see him in **a department store and** he asked for my autograph.
>
> **—Shirley Temple**

mary steenburgen

I had a pacifier I was quite fond of, and my mother called on Santa to try and make me get rid of it. I was about three years old and I received a letter from Santa saying there was another little girl who really needed a pacifier, and that if I left my pacifier for Santa, he'd give me a doll.

jamie-lynn sigler

Holidays were a big ordeal in my house. My father is Jewish, so we'd have a menorah and a Hanukkah party. But we also celebrated Christmas. One Hanukkah party, I was given a card with a picture of Santa on it, and inside Santa's long white beard was a picture of a white puppy. "Well, where is it?" I yelped. And it was upstairs in the kitchen. It was really exciting because a pet was all I wanted for as long as I can remember. I mean, I even had an imaginary dog for a while.

susan lucci

There was a sale in my town, called the White Elephant Sale, to raise money for our school, and it was all secondhand stuff. It was Valentine's Day and this boy bought me a doll and a bracelet at the sale. He also gave me all his Little League patches. My father came home, saw the gifts, and insisted I give them all back. The boy was ten years old and my dad called his dad and told him what his son was spending his allowance on. My dad was embarrassed, but he thought it was the right thing.

My birthday is December 23. December 22 was the night my parents put up the tree and the lights. Then, on the morning of the twenty-third, I'd get my birthday presents under the Christmas tree. I appreciated that they tried to make it special for me. My mom would say to my grandma, "It's not Susan's fault she was born on the twenty-third."

I remember Christmas as a magical time. My father would read me "The Night Before Christmas." My grandmother lived with us until I was eleven. She was wonderful in the kitchen. She was amazing—she would sit there with a bowl and whip chocolate cupcakes up from scratch. To this day, I make chocolate cupcakes at Christmas. Except mine are Duncan Hines. They're still good, but it's not the same thing.

kathy najimy

Almost every holiday was at one of my grandparents'
houses. There'd be tons and tons of Lebanese food.
Like on Thanksgiving, we'd have tabbouleh and
hummus and rolled grape leaves. It's the greatest
food in the world. We'd put long tables on the patio
or we'd go to the beach and put up umbrellas.
Fourth of July, New Year's . . . there'd be a million kids
running around. We'd be in our little bathing suits.
God love me, I always had the bathing suit with the
little shorts—a chubby bathing suit.

chris evert

One Christmas, I swear I saw
Santa Claus in the hallway. It
couldn't have actually happened,
because my parents would never
have dressed up, but in my mind, I
saw him coming out of my parents'
bedroom. It almost made me believe again.

kathy najimy

My favorite candies were Milk Duds and Black Cow Suckers, which were caramel lollipop sticks dipped in chocolate. I loved winner suckers too. They were just like lollipops, but if you opened the wrapper and it said *winner* inside, you got to get another free sucker.

lisa ling

My father is very farsighted. Bursting open our fortune cookies was always fun. My father would put on his glasses and read his out loud: "I am very fortunate to have such good daughters." Of course it never really said that. He's a very sweet man.

It's so **beautifully arranged** on the plate— you know someone's fingers have been all over it.

—Julia Child

gladys knight

My favorite after-school snack was Krispy Kreme doughnuts and a carton of milk. I'd buy them at lunchtime and put them in my book bag, only to forget about them until the walk home. By then they'd be all smashed up.

ellen burstyn

I loved those pink, black, and white candy squares. The black part was licorice and I don't know what the other parts were. They made a mess of your mouth, but I just loved them.

mary steenburgen

My favorite Thanksgiving dish was my mom's sweet potatoes with melted marshmallows and melted Red Hots on top. Don't knock it until you try it.

jane **pratt**

My favorite after-school snack was Pixie Sticks, the powder that you put on your hand.

cherry jones

As a girl the first thing I did when I came home from school was grab a Coca-Cola, saltines, and cheddar cheese (a lot of it!), then head outside and get in the trees.

The Sixties

I WORE
Black tights with loafers
Black turtleneck sweaters
Espadrilles
Long ironed hair
Bell-bottoms
Miniskirts

I ATE/DRANK
TV dinners
Fiddle Faddle
Tang
Rice-A-Roni
Fritos corn chips
Dippy Canoes
Shake 'n Bake
Hostess snacks
Brach's candy
Howard Johnson's pistachio
    ice cream
Moon Pies
Hi-C fruit drink

I DANCED
The Jitterbug
The Bus Stop
The Twist
The Monkey

I WORSHIPED
Grace Kelly
Eddie Fisher
Gene Kelly
Fabian
Tuesday Weld
Suzy Parker
Natalie Wood
The Beatles

My look is attainable. Women can look like Audrey Hepburn by flipping out their hair, buying the large sunglasses, and the little sleeveless dresses.

—Audrey Hepburn

I WATCHED
Gidget movies
Where the Boys Are
American Bandstand
The Mod Squad
Gilligan's Island
The Addams Family
Batman

I LISTENED TO
Frankie Avalon
Connie Francis
Pete Seeger
The Weavers
The Beatles
Bob Dylan
Tom Jones

I READ

Betsy-Tacy and Tib books

Tiger Beat magazine

16 magazine

Rolling Stone

Dick and Jane readers

Valley of the Dolls by Jacqueline
    Susann

Harriet the Spy by Louise Fitzhugh

The Phantom Tollbooth by Norton
    Juster

I USED

Shalimar perfume

Maybelline makeup

Yardley soap

Noxzema

Lifebuoy soap

Breck hair spray

Prell shampoo

The Sixties

anna quindlen

ANNA QUINDLEN

I lived in the most wonderful neighborhood, this suburb of Philadelphia that's filled with oldish but not really old houses built in the '20s and '30s. There were all these wonderful flowers in the springtime. There were great azaleas and rhododendrons, mimosa trees and lilac bushes. When I was in Philadelphia on business about five years ago, I did that thing that one ought never do, which is to go back to the old neighborhood. I expected it to be diminished and completely different from what I remembered. In fact, it was just the same.

When I was really little I used to run away a lot—far enough so that my mother was worried, but not so far that she couldn't easily find me and haul me back home. I would get on my bike and wind up at my aunt and uncle's house, a substantial-distance-across-a-number-of-busy-roads-away and get in trouble for that. I was always very, very outspoken. I talked all the time. I had a casual attitude toward the truth. I didn't back down from it. When I was very little I used to insist that there were lions and tigers down the street. I think I had—even then—the soul of a fiction writer.

We didn't have a front porch, but all the kids in my neighborhood were outside all the time in the evening. We were always out in the street playing "monkey in the middle" or "kick the can." Many a lightning bug met an untimely death in the bottom of a jar without enough holes punched in the top. All of my girlfriends lived within a five-block area of us; our school was about five or six blocks away, so we all walked to school together: I lived the farthest away, so I started. Then I picked up Janet; then I picked up Donna; and you knew Debbie would be coming from the other direction so we'd meet her on the street in front of school.

We had a lot of pets. We had cats who were always having kittens. And for some reason we always had white mice. And since my mother was always pregnant, she frequently walked around with a mouse in the front pocket of her maternity smock. I remember thinking it was unremarkable, but sometimes when my mother would come to the door, this little mouse head would peek above the edge of the maternity smock and someone would scream.

If there was something sexual we were fascinated and repelled by—like French kissing—I'd be deputized to go and ask my mom about it.

My mother had two faces. She had her everyday face and she had her going-out face. Her everyday face was very strong and—if I didn't know her—maybe a little intimidating. She had a very strong rounded nose, very black eyes, and very black hair. Her nighttime face was incredibly glamorous, because with the very black hair and the very black eyes, she wore very red lipstick, very white powder, and very black mascara—and a little cake makeup. My mother, when she was dressed up, always wore black. I was never permitted to wear black when I was a girl. Which may be why I wear it all the time now. I just thought she was incredibly glam. I don't think my mother ever saw herself that way. She was actually a quiet woman, sort of self-effacing.

My father was the big personality; my mother was the straight man. As a child I remember thinking that she was sort of perfect.

My girlfriends always thought my mom was cool. My mom was the mom who told us stuff. My mom was the mom who told us about getting your period. If there was something sexual we were fascinated and repelled by—like French kissing—I'd be deputized to go and ask my mom about it. She was very good at understanding what children needed and giving it to them even if it didn't always meet her comfort level. She would tell me what we needed to know and I would come back to the playground and everyone would go *Ooooooh* and *Ahhhhhhh*.

My first best friend was my best friend all through school. Her name was Donna and she chose me in third grade. I can't remember, I think it was one of those chemical reactions that was utterly right, because Donna is a very grounded, no-nonsense, down-to-earth person. She is the middle child in a family of nine; I am the oldest child in a family of five. I was much more fanciful and out there, and so we meshed perfectly. She's a person, even now, who is utterly and completely dependable, the kind of person I think I really needed in my life.

For most of my childhood,
I was either Queen Anna or
I was being dethroned,
one or the other.
Two very different experiences
that basically teach you
everything you need to know
for the rest of
your life in the world.

It's so interesting watching my daughter, who is a person with a really big personality. I said once if personalities had colors hers would be red. One day, one of the mothers of her friends called me to say, "I think I should tell you something I heard today. One of the boys said, 'This year let's dethrone Queen Maria.'" And it was as though my whole childhood passed before my eyes. Because for most of my childhood, I was either Queen Anna or I was being dethroned. One or the other. Two very different experiences that basically teach you everything you need to know for the rest of your life in the world.

My first memory of loss was not of death, it was of moving. We moved when I was at the end of my eighth-grade year. I had grown up in that neighborhood. I knew everyone in the neighborhood. They all knew me. I had this very close circle of friends. I remember realizing that someone else was going to live in our house. It made me—throughout the rest of my life—never want to move except when it was absolutely, positively, incontrovertibly necessary.

friends

I am treating you as
my friend,
asking you to share my present
minuses in the hope
I can ask you to share
my future pluses.

—Katherine Mansfield

my best friend

mary steenburgen

I loved to play with my best friend, Tommy. He was my next-door neighbor, and every morning I'd go over to his house. He had this big box of hats and we would close our eyes, pick a hat, and whichever hat we picked, that's who we were going to be that day. We were firemen or policemen or pilots. I started acting with him at a very young age.

I've got a friend down there.

Or at least a potential friend.

Do you know what it's like to have a friend? . . .

That wasn't supposed to be a stumper.

—Buffy, *Buffy the Vampire Slayer*

Tommy and I had really wild imaginations. We would run loose in the woods, and I remember one time we were playing cowboys and Indians, and we tied a neighbor, this boy Lee, up to a tree, and we forgot about him. At the end of the night, when all the mothers came home and called their kids inside, we heard someone hollering, "Lee," and we remembered, "Oh my god! Lee's tied to a tree!"

dee dee myers

My sisters were my first best girlfriends. We moved around a lot, so even if we didn't know anybody, we had each other, and we could conspire against our parents together, which is very important. At school, I always had a ton of friends. Of course, there were times when I felt outside of my group. I remember that angst—trying to figure out where you fit in, who you are, where you're going, how you're the same, and whether it's okay to be different.

fionnula flanagan

My best friend when I was ten years old—I can see her so vividly in front of my eyes—her name was Eileen. Her father was a magician at the Capital Theater and, of course, that to me was wonderful. She wore her hair in a short brown bob with a very large white or pink bow. Her father used to bring her things from England when he went there to tour as a magician. So I was envious of her at the same time as I loved her. We had many secrets together.

At that age one wants a companion in crime.

Most of our secrets involved vowing that we would always be friends and we still are, actually. We pledged to live together, to do everything together, to dress in certain ways together. At that age one wants a companion in crime.

I think the worst thing we ever did involved another young girl the same age. Her name was Dolores and she was this teacher's pet and she was perfect at sewing. In our sewing class, we were given small pieces of immaculately white cotton to take home over the weekends and asked to make buttonholes.

So one day, in a total rage, we stole Dolores's buttonholes and ripped them to shreds in the girls' toilet.

Dolores could sew a perfect buttonhole, as if she'd spent the weekend in a convent stitching, while mine looked like a spider escaped from an inkwell and walked all over the cotton. They were filthy and horrible and I hated it. Eileen's weren't much better. So one day, in a total rage, we stole Dolores's buttonholes and ripped them to shreds in the girls' toilet. I never would have confessed to that; now the secret is out! We got in terrible trouble for it too.

jane pratt

I grew up not trusting romantic love. I saw it as something that fizzled out. I trusted family love—that, no matter what, my dad was always going to love me, and I was always going to love my mom, and she was always going to love my brother.

We put on those rope bracelets and said we were never going to take them off, and it felt permanent.

And my love with my best girlfriend, that felt permanent. We put on those rope bracelets and said we were never going to take them off, and it felt permanent.

kelly preston

Living in Hawaii, I hung out on the beach a lot. It was very natural and fun and very casual. I wore my bikini all the time. I was very much an outdoor kid. I had a best friend, Simone, and we and a bunch of girls—Shelley and Kelly, Carey and Marian—were a gang. We would skateboard all of the time, doing the tandem thing, where you go down the vacant freeway at forty miles an hour and crash into the side rails. Simone and I would play in forts and have these cool wars.

alex kingston

My best friend was Jane and she had eczema and asthma. She was quite petite, very nice, a lovely girl. I think I had a mad imagination, so we were always playing fantasy games. We would act out "Hansel and Gretel" or "Rose Red." I would always have to be the lead. I always wanted to play the beautiful one.

If we played *Heidi*, Jane would always have to play Peter, poor girl.

So Jane would have to play the boy, the prince or, if we played *Heidi*, Jane would always have to play Peter, poor girl. We'd put a ladder up against a chest of drawers and pretend it was a mountain. And we'd sleep under the ladder. That would be our home.

candace bushnell

when i was a girl ...

I grew up in a little town called Glastonbury, Connecticut, and there was a lot of farmland. It was a pretty WASPy town. It was very upper middle class; everybody played tennis; everybody was on the swim team. I was forced to be on the swim team at the age of four, which actually wasn't that great because we had to get up at six in the morning. Summer mornings, I'd have to be up for swim meets to dive into a freezing cold pool and swim ten laps. It wasn't very pleasant, but everybody did it.

Glastonbury was a town where people dressed the same and looked the same. If you didn't know somebody, you recognized them because they looked just like "Joe" from your school. Everybody knew each other. Everybody knew what everybody else was up to. People would go to the club on weekends and have cookouts and that kind of thing.

On those cold, snowy, winter
school days when we
had the day off,
our parents would open the door
and send us outside.
And they expected us to stay out.
If you came back with a little bit
of frostbite, tough luck.

It was ideal for a kid. There were lots
of other kids, and we just never spent time
with our parents—or being supervised by our
parents. On those cold, snowy, winter school
days when we had the day off, our parents
would open the door and send us outside.
And they expected us to stay out. If you came
back with a little bit of frostbite it was tough
luck. So it was a very New England kind of
town, Norman Rockwell, traditional. Nobody's
mother worked. Everyone's mother stayed
home and cleaned the house and talked on
the phone.

"Mom, can I get a peanut butter
sandwich?"

"Quiet! I'm on the phone with Betty!"

I think as a kid I was often looking
around thinking, *God, how did I end up here?*

CANDACE BUSHNELL

I'm probably one of the few people in America who actually had a good childhood, but I always knew I was going to get out of there. I never planned to stay in that small town; I was always looking at it with an eye of not being there forever.

My sister and I were always telling stories. We had costumes and marionettes and we were always putting on little plays for the neighborhood. My sister and I, every night, would take turns telling stories. Starting from when I was eight, I told everybody that I was going to be a writer. I think it was a strange thing to say because in the town I grew up in, we didn't know anybody who was a writer. There was a woman who lived next door who wrote for the *Glastonbury Citizen*, but I think her husband owned the paper. That was the extent of any kind of publishing world in our town.

I'm probably one of the few people in America who actually had a good childhood, but I always knew I was going to get out of there. I never planned to stay in that small town; I was always looking at it with an eye of not being there forever.

I remember the moment I knew I'd be a writer. It was an epiphany moment. I was sitting in the classroom reading a book and in the book it was snowing. I looked outside and it was a beautiful spring day and I thought, *But I expected it to be snowing!* I was so into the book, I'd been so transported, I thought it'd be snowing outside. It was the most powerful thing. I wanted to do that too. And I thought, *Someday, you are going to be a novelist.* Thirty years later, here I am.

play

rita moreno

There was a doll that I really loved. I think I named her Rosita. My mother brought her for me from America. And it was my first inkling that there were people who were fair-skinned with blue eyes and blond hair. In fact, I don't think I ever saw a doll with dark hair or olive skin. That would be something to aspire to, later on in life, which would eventually get me into a lot of emotional trouble.

amy sedaris

I played with Barbie dolls a lot. I was obsessed with them. I played with them until I was too old to play with them. I had the whole Barbie house and I loved buying clothes and shoes for her.

I knew Barbie had a good body, but it never made me think I had to have a body like that. Now they have a Barbie that comes in a wheelchair. Her name's Becky, and she doesn't fit in Barbie's playhouse, which is hilarious. If I was a kid, I would love that: You have a cripple Barbie, but Barbie's house doesn't have ramps or anything. "Hey! We're all going to the beach. Sorry, Becky, you can't go. . . ." It's so mean.

"What I believe about dolls," she said, "is that they can do things they will not let us know about. Perhaps, really, Emily can read and talk and walk, but she will only do it when people are out of the room. That is her secret."

—Sarah Crewe, *A Little Princess* by **Frances Hodgson Burnett**

denyce graves

When I was in the third grade, I was really good at double Dutch. There was this kid in our class named Larry. Now this was third grade, and Larry was sixteen. Okay? Sixteen! He belonged to a juvenile detention center that sent him there. He hadn't advanced grades. Larry was the boss. He ruled the third grade. And one day, we were playing jump rope outside and I was going to jump, when a pretty girl in the class, Tania, said, "No, I don't want to turn. I want to keep jumping!"

It was terrible. They all beat me up, and I looked horrible.

And I said, "Well, it's my turn to jump," but she wanted to keep jumping, and eventually I threw the ropes down and said, "I am not going to turn." She went and told Larry, who told everybody, "We are going to get Denyce after class today." And so I went and told my third-grade teacher, Mr. Rockefeller. I adored Mr. Rockefeller. He had a purple piano, he made up songs, and he used to give us chocolate-covered malt balls. Anyway, I told him that everybody was going to beat me up, so he let me stay after class and help him wash and beat the erasers.

I waited until about three forty-five and then I went home. And there everybody was. They were at my apartment waiting for me. Even my boyfriend, Terry, was there. It was terrible. They all beat me up, and I looked horrible.

kathy najimy

When I was about eight years old, we had a group we called the "Act So Smart Club." Growing up in San Diego, I found that there was really one way for a girl to look, and that was to be thin with long blond hair parted in the middle. If you weren't that, you were basically an alternative-type person. So I gathered up all the sort of misfits on the street and we became the Act So Smart Club.

I made myself president—I mean, where else would I get voted president?

We had a basement in our house that I was not allowed to go in, because it was full of chipped wood and rusty nails and broken glass that had been left from the people who lived there before us. The Act So Smart Club found it challenging to go into the basement without running scared. We were always sure there was someone down there, or that we'd find the clues to some horrendous crime. We were always looking for crimes, though we never committed any ourselves.

fionnula flanagan

I know this sounds tremendously morbid, but when I was a girl, we used to play hanging games. We used to hang all my dolls in the backyard from a tree; then we'd bury them and have a funeral.

Funeral games were great because you could get dressed up and wear hats and bring flowers.

Funeral games were great because you could get dressed up and wear hats and bring flowers and make speeches at the grave site. I am sure, to this day, that those dolls are still buried in that garden.

candace bushnell

My friends and I had these Wicca-type rituals. We had this scheme to kill a boy in the neighborhood. We were going to make a cake out of mud, which we'd save for the winter. Then we'd cover it with snow and feed it to him. I don't know where we got this from.

lee ann womack

When I was a girl, the toy I wanted more than anything was a go-cart. I never got it. Now I'm glad my parents denied me. I was too irresponsible for that toy.

elizabeth perkins

I tended to get into trouble a lot. I would steal things from neighbors' yards or give the cat a bath with Clorox bleach or steal my sister's Barbie dolls and take their heads off and bury them in the backyard.

If a boy hit me,
I hit him back twice as hard.

I didn't act the way girls are supposed to act. If a boy hit me, I hit him back twice as hard. And that wasn't the way you were supposed to act. You were supposed to sit with your napkin in your lap and you weren't supposed to respond and if you did, you had to do it politely. I was very feisty and confident and I wasn't going to take any grief from anybody. They'd say, "She's gonna be dark when she grows up."

tanya tucker

The toy I wanted more than anything else was a Susie Homemaker Oven, and I never got one. To this day, my parents feel bad about it. They've never forgiven themselves for denying me something to bake my mud pies in.

mary steenburgen

I had this birthday party when I was nine years old, and my friends and I were having a séance and we tried to call upon the spirit of Lee Harvey Oswald. He was, in our young minds, just about the vilest person you can think of. I remember, whoever was leading the trance declared, "If the spirit of Lee Harvey Oswald is in this room let his presence be known!" Unbeknownst to us, my mother had snuck into the room. At that most crucial moment, she hit the lowest note on our piano, scaring the daylights out of us. One girl turned completely white and she was halfway down the road before we could stop her. We were all in hysterics. It was paralyzing, it was terrifying. But I was so proud of my mother for being so cool and funny, I got over it.

joan chen

When I was a girl in Shanghai, we experienced a certain deprivation; we experienced political losses. But I feel like that forced me to play in a way that was more imaginative and creative. I lived in a great community, and I was like a free-run chicken.

Shanghai is usually kind of cloudy, and on a sunny day, the kids were sent down to occupy the trees so the family would have space to air-dry their clothes. I remember so very well the smell of washed sheets air-dried in the sun. I told my husband, "The dryer's great, but there's no smell like the sun." He said, "What? The sun doesn't have a smell!" But it does; it really does.

It was as if she were telling me, "That's the end of your doll-playing years."

We had very few toys, and I remember making origami and doing simple woodwork. I had this one doll I cherished, and we were playing near a construction site. There was all this sand, and we had a bucket, and I left my doll—the first and last doll I'd have—I left it there. I was devastated.

I remember my mother saying, "There you go, you lost it!" It was as if she were telling me, "That's the end of your doll-playing years."

cynthia nixon

when i was a girl . . .

I was not a rebellious kind of person. I felt bad that I wasn't. In the movie *One True Thing,* Meryl Streep's character talks about the heroines in books who are spunky and outspoken—like Jo March in *Little Women* or that girl in *My Brilliant Career.* These were girls who didn't want to marry, who spoke up for people. She compares herself to them, and that's how I always felt. *Oh, I'm boring. I'm Meg. Who wants to be Meg? No one wants to be Meg!*

As a child, I was much more comfortable with adults than kids. I knew they would talk to me, whereas with kids, there was the fear, *Are they gonna reject me?* I would just not even try a lot of the time. I was shy, I think.

I was alone a lot, and I think I liked being alone. It surprised my mother, how much alone time I seemed to need. I remember playing for hours with dolls. I had these paper dolls of little girls—one was a ballerina, one was a figure skater, and one was a model. And I would play with these for hours and hours. Some people have an imaginary friend, but I had an imaginary daughter. Her name was Malka Bolmer and she lived in California. At some point, I had a cardboard hut in the corner of my room. It was like a secret hideout place and I remember loving that so much. I think there's something so precious to a kid about a closet, or a small little space that they can crawl into. Maybe it's because kids are so little and the world seems so big, and to be in a little nook is a very magical thing.

My mother went back to work when I was one month old. She was very much a career woman. I juggle things more than she did: I'm with my daughter a lot, and then I'm at work. I think when she was at work, she was at work. And when she came home, she gave herself over to that. She and I didn't spend a lot of time doing the domestic arts. She indoctrinated me into doing things she thought were fun—like going to see plays or movies or singing show tunes. There was a sense of adventure—we would go and do things more than stay at home and do projects.

My mother seemed to have endless room for me.
My father, not so much.

CYNTHIA NIXON

My mother seemed to have endless room for me. My father, not so much, particularly after they separated. My father would have me for a day or two; sometimes, on vacation, he might have me for a week. He'd always hit this "I need to go be with grown-ups" point. This was a shocking thing for me. My mother would always say, "You're the best company in the world." She thought of me as a buddy, as another adult. I think my father took taking care of a child much more seriously. He was often trying to improve me.

My mother had been an actress, and she took me to see many plays and movies from a very early age. We would always dissect them afterward. We'd talk about why a particular actress's performance was good, why it wasn't, how it could have been better. I think it was then that the seed was planted. At first, I did a bit of modeling, an appearance on a game show, little things, and by the time I was nine I was telling people I was going to be an actress. When I was twelve I started working professionally. In high school I was hopeful I would be an actor, but I wasn't sure. And I wasn't really, really sure I was going to be an actor until I graduated from college and became a full-fledged adult.

I went to a very rigorous public high school. You had to test many times to get into it. People were very smart, and they had these extremely divergent and impressive interests and hobbies and projects and skills.

I really loved high school. I would say it's really the centerpiece of my life. That sounds pathetic, but it wasn't.

I really loved high school. I would say it's really the centerpiece of my life. That sounds pathetic, but it wasn't. Not only did I have one best friend, I had ten. There was a pack of us and we had such interesting discussions. We had a lot of homework, but we would hang out endlessly. We'd play ultimate Frisbee, hang out at the candy shop, or hang out at each other's houses, and have impassioned discussions about our parents' psychology. It was a great time.

I felt so centered in my group of friends. I felt they were really helping to give me another point of view. I was very much my mother's daughter, and I learned so much of who I was from her, and here were these people I could learn almost as much from. They had different points of view, and that was so confusing and interesting and exciting all at once.

CYNTHIA NIXON

When I graduated from high school, I felt more on a track than most people. I had six years of professional experience under my belt, money in the bank, and experience in the workplace. I didn't know if I was going to be able to make the transition to being an adult actor, but as opposed to kids who didn't know what they wanted to do, I think I was relatively assured.

I think it was senior year in high school; our social studies teacher went around the room and asked us what would make us happy in life. I said I wanted things to continue exactly as they were. I wanted to work, to have these friends, and live in New York. I just wanted it to continue.

the world
beyond
my backyard

wendie
malick

The world beyond my backyard was represented by New York City. The first time my parents took me there, I was six. I saw my first Broadway musical, *The Unsinkable Molly Brown*. My sister and brother conked out at intermission. They went back to the hotel with my father, and my mom and I stayed until the end. She took me to Lindy's for cheesecake, and I remember thinking, *This is the world I belong in, this is the world I want to have*. Buffalo was too small for me. I knew from my first moment of real consciousness that I couldn't wait to get to New York City.

I knew from my first moment of real consciousness that I couldn't wait to get to New York City.

marian wright edelman

Growing up, the world beyond my backyard seemed
available to me. As long as we had books, as long as
we had the Bible, as long as we had imaginative people. . . . We were lucky—I was lucky!—because my parents traveled and my grandparents lived in New
York, so we drove there and we saw things. I can't
ever remember a time, living in that little segregated
town, that I was not aware there was a big world out
there. We talked about India, we talked about foreign
policy, and so the world felt both near and far. We
didn't have a television, but we listened to the news
on the radio. I was so happy to have parents with
whom I could discuss things, who were sharing the
struggles and the challenges that were going on. I
look back and it takes my breath away to think of the
courage of all these black parents in Clarington,
South Carolina. I have seen transforming changes,
and I have seen that it has come not from people
who are in the mainstream but from the margins.

What a
wonderful life I've had!
I only wish I'd
realized it sooner.

—Colette

michelle rodriguez

When I turned eight and had moved to a city, my backyard was filled with blocks and blocks of people to meet, things to do, bikes to ride, songs to sing. I realized that the world out there needed to be confronted . . . I just had to go out there and throw myself in it and just have it take me over. I'm just a messenger, man. I just take it all in and throw it back out. I think that is the purpose of life. So far anyway. That might change. Everything does.

elizabeth perkins

The world beyond my own backyard seemed like Oz, like that moment where Dorothy opens the door after the house falls and everything that was once in black and white is now in color.

The world beyond my own backyard seemed like Oz.

I thought there was going to be a yellow brick road, that I'd follow it, and end up in the Emerald City. And I couldn't wait to open that door. I knew that if I stayed in the small town that I was living in, there would be no way that I was going to be happy. I had to see what was out there.

cynthia nixon

When I was seven, we moved from New York City's
West Side to the East Side. On the West Side, we
lived in the high nineties. It was the height of the
recession; the neighborhood had a slightly dangerous feeling; there was a lot of hanging out on
stoops. When we moved to the East Side, no one
would sit out on the stoop. There
were no stoops! It wasn't
the fancy East Side, it
was Yorkville, but it
was still proper.

I WORE

Dingo boots
Olaf Daughter clogs
Nikes
Rainbow suspenders
Earth shoes
Eight-inch Afros
Danskins
Sears Tuffskins
Coral necklaces
Macramé anklets

I ATE/DRANK

Chico-sticks
David's sunflower seeds
Lemon drops
Pringles
Pixie Sticks
Fun Dip
Pop Rocks

I DANCED

The Bump
The Double Bump
The L.A. Cha Cha
The Hustle

I WORSHIPED

John Travolta
Andrea McArdle
Shaun Cassidy
Nadia Comaneci
Dorothy Hamill
Jodie Foster
Tatum O'Neal
Tracy Austin
Billie Jean King
Tamara Dobson (Cleopatra
    Jones)
Cher
David Bowie
Chris Evert
Diana Ross
Parker Stevenson

You can't just sit there and wait for people to give you that golden dream. You've got to get out there and make it happen for yourself.

—Diana Ross

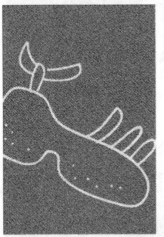

I WATCHED

Charlie's Angels

The Bionic Woman

Wonder Woman

Sonny and Cher

Sanford and Son

American Bandstand

Soul Train

Saturday morning cartoons on ABC

The Partridge Family

The Donny and Marie Show

The Captain and Tenille Show

Little House on the Prairie

Welcome Back, Kotter

All in the Family

Mary Tyler Moore

Rhoda

I LISTENED TO

The Carpenters
The Rolling Stones
Linda Ronstadt
Fleetwood Mac
James Brown
Diana Ross
Cher
David Bowie
Carole King
Carly Simon

I READ

Dynamite! magazine
Bananas magazine
Dreams Die First by
    Harold Robbins
Hollywood by Rona Barrett

I USED

Nivea lotion
Stridex
Noxzema
Bonne Bell
Love's Baby Soft
Jean Naté
Nair (for short shorts)
Tame conditioner
Body on Tap

The Seventies

ann curry

when i was a girl...

My mother would have described me as loud.
You know, LOUD. She'd say, "Anna, how come
you talk so loud? Be like a lady, Anna." My
mom was a Japanese woman from the old
country. She had this stoic and elegant way
about her, and here I was, encouraged by the
times, to be a GIRL. She dreamed of having a
daughter who loved pink and ruffles and lace,
a Lawrence Welk girl. Instead, she got this
rough-and-tumble, I-want-to-play-softball-get-
outta-my-way-boys kind of a girl.

My parents couldn't have been more
different from each other. She was four foot
eleven; he was six foot three. She came from a
poor rice farmer family in rural Japan; he
came from a poor Scottish Irish family in
Pueblo, Colorado. The one thing they had in
common was growing up with financial odds.
They met on a streetcar during the occupa-
tion of Japan fresh after the war. He couldn't
believe how beautiful she was, punching the
tickets. He would get on the streetcar and

ride it and ride it, waiting to get up the courage to ask her out for noodles. He barely spoke Japanese, she barely spoke English, but there was a language between them. They suffered a lot of discrimination. The military actually sent him away to Morocco to prevent them from getting married; it was only because he refused to give up that they eventually got back together.

I'd gotten to the point where life had become an adventure, and moving offered all the possibilities of reinventing myself, of meeting new people, of seeing the world through a different group of friends.

My father was a career navy man, so we moved around a lot. I think the longest time we ever lived in one place was four years and that was Norfolk, Virginia. I think it is very destabilizing for a child to move around a lot, but it got to a point where I actually looked forward to going elsewhere. I remember, I was just ending junior high school, and I was leaving Norfolk, Virginia. My girlfriend came over, crying, "Ann, I don't want you to go!" I looked at her and I realized that she was hurt that I

wasn't crying. It made me feel broken that I
didn't feel what she felt. I went up to my
room—now completely empty—and thought,
*How could I possibly leave Kim Davis and not
be upset?* Then I burst into tears. I came
downstairs, really unhappy with myself, and
she looked so relieved to see these tears in
my eyes. Of course I was going to miss her
too. But I'd gotten to the point where life had
become an adventure, and moving offered all
the possibilities of reinventing myself, of
meeting new people, of seeing the world
through a different group of friends.

My father had expected me to be a
boy, but he never treated me in a girly way.
He'd say stuff to me like, "Ann, go out and
show 'em what a Curry can do. I see a spark in
you, Ann, I see a light." He wanted me to go
out and be of service. "If you do that," he
said, "you'll know—at the end of your days—
that your life mattered." My dad and I would
watch Walter Cronkite pretty much every
night. At the dinner table, he would get pas-
sionate about the news of the day. Invariably,
he'd end up pounding his fist on the dinner
table. I'd be mid-bite and he'd be yelling,
"What's wrong with our young people today?"
Or "What is this stuff about protesting
against the Vietnam war?"

My brothers
and sisters would pick up
their plates and
leave the dinner table
because Ann and Dad were
going to have at it.

I'd say, "Well, Dad, maybe they have a point. What are we doing in Vietnam?" And his eyes would grow big and my brothers and sisters would pick up their plates and leave the dinner table because Ann and Dad were going to have at it. We fought about it all—women's rights, civil rights—and he'd egg me on, push me, make me get so upset that my face would get red and I'd start sweating. But in the end, he'd always say, "Ann, I don't always agree with you, but I would still vote for you for president." To this day he still asks me when I'm going to run for president.

This one boy, Butch,
got up in front of the
class and yelled,
 "Ann is a Jap! Ann is a
  Jap! Ann is a Jap!"
Over and over again
and he wouldn't stop.
All the kids were
watching me to see
what I'd do, and
I stood up, hauled back,
 and slugged him
  straight in the teeth.

ANN CURRY

I got teased as a child. And it got ugly.
This one boy, Butch, got up in front of the
class and yelled, "Ann is a Jap! Ann is a Jap!
Ann is a Jap!" Over and over again and he
wouldn't stop. All the kids were watching me
to see what I'd do, and I stood up, hauled
back, and slugged him straight in the teeth. He
fell on the ground, blood gushing, screaming,
crying. The teacher came running in. I was
completely ashamed and aghast at what I had

done. He got sent to the principal's office, I got sent to the front of the room. She never said a word to me, never chastised me. Here, I'd slugged that kid. I might have even loosened a tooth or two. Yet, she admonished him instead of me. I think she created a space in me that said "It's okay to stick up for yourself."

All in all, I think I was a pretty fearless child. I can't remember being afraid of anything. My sister was scared of the dark, and I remember walking her to the bathroom at night because she was too scared to do it herself. I'm not sure if I had to be strong for everyone else, or that's just how I was. I think it was my father who instilled much of my confidence in me. I remember the first time I got straight A's on a report card, he gave me a dictionary as a gift. It was a thick, big, red book and it was all mine.

I signed my name in it: "Ann Curry, November 20th, 1968." Then, years later in 1975, after I graduated high school, I wrote, "Still have a lot to learn." Then, in 1987, I added, "Thank you for this book of words, Dad." I have gone back to this book many times, remembering how much it meant to me. No one in the family had gone to college, by giving me this dictionary, it felt like my father was giving me the world.

It's still in my office, this dictionary. It's my greatest treasure, my greatest reward.

school

Prejudices, it is well known,

are most difficult to eradicate from

the heart whose soil

has never been

loosened or

fertilized by education.

—Charlotte Brontë

school

ellen burstyn

There was a girl who wrote in my yearbook, "To the girl who could get away with anything . . ." I remember reading that and having no idea people saw me like that. Yes, I was captain of the cheerleaders and president of the student council and the drama club. And, yes, I was pretty popular in school. So while I may have been viewed as an outgoing happy person, inside I felt lonely and not at all confident. I guess I put on a good show.

> # No one can make you
> ## feel inferior without
> ## your consent.
> **—Eleanor Roosevelt**

anna quindlen

I really like to stick up for nuns. And I am going to stick up for nuns here, because I was educated by an order of nuns. They weren't the kind of nuns who hit you over the knuckles with rulers. They seemed to me very smart and very capable, and not in the least dependent on men to do things. They lived together in the convent next to our school, and I was really impressed by them, but sort of terrified too. There were one or two who goaded me to rise to the level they thought I could attain—it made a huge difference in my life. My mother was surrounded by all these little kids; she had five kids in ten years, so she was either pregnant, or with a baby, or chasing one around. And here were these women who lived these lives of perfect order and intellectual pursuit. Between school and home, I was able to envision the many roles women could play.

illeana douglas

I grew up in a very small community and it was somewhat idyllic in that there were a lot of musicians and
artists around. I'd say I got my first taste of the real
world when, unfortunately, I entered school. My life
before school was: Today we're gonna paint pictures
and ride horses, wear costumes and hats, and sing
and dance. And it was stopped dead cold. All of a
sudden there were all these rules.

I hate to say that it was school that did me in,
but that's kind of what happened. I remember feeling,
*Wow, there are all these rules, and, whoa, I can't fol-
low all this.* The summer between third and fourth
grade, I taught myself how to write script. And then,
in school the next year, the penmanship teacher
pulled my book away from me, showed it to the
class, and put a big F on it. I'd been pretty creative
with my cursive, and she was telling me not to be.
*You're supposed to do it the way I tell you to do it.
Don't be creative,* was the message I got.

**Everybody wanted to look like
Christie Brinkley, and I wanted to look
like Nastassja Kinski or Liza Minnelli
from *Cabaret*.**

After that, I wrote a satirical poem about her and had it published in the newspaper. She was very upset and wanted it to be taken out, and I think that was my first example of using humor as a way to get a point across.

In high school, there was this clique of girls—they were sort of like the wealthy cheerleader kinds of girls, the ones that you would anticipate being mean. I was of Italian descent, and there weren't very many dark people in our class. Everybody else was Protestant-, Irish-, English-, or Scottish-looking and, because I didn't look like everybody else, I got teased. I wasn't able to afford the latest clothes. Everybody wanted to look like Christie Brinkley, and I wanted to look like Nastassja Kinski or Liza Minnelli from *Cabaret*. That didn't really fit in our high school.

elizabeth perkins

High school was very dramatic for me. I was very much an outcast. I was the one they called weird. I think on a lot of levels, I embraced that. Weird behavior becomes the shell that you live in; it protects you. I was all this crazy unfocused energy. I knew there was a place for me somewhere, but it definitely wasn't the school I was in.

gillian anderson

There are lots of opportunities for regret, but there is only one thing I truly wish I'd been more mindful of, and that's studying, listening in class. There are huge gaps in my knowledge of history, geography, just everything. I grew up in London, then came to the States to go to school: I was just a conglomeration of ignorance.

I was just a conglomeration of ignorance.

I was always wanting attention: I'd put worms in teachers' shoes and gum and glue, shaving cream in the drawer, and talked constantly. I passed notes. I was the one—while the teacher's back was turned—who organized the class to drop their books on the floor all at once. I was just a nightmare.

And then all of a sudden, out of left field, a woman, an English teacher who used to visit me when I was on house detention, gave me the impression she saw something in me. And that stopped me dead in my tracks. This was in tenth grade, I think, and I auditioned for a community play, and that's when everything changed for me. All of a sudden I was performing, I was directing. The world opened up.

The kids I'd been grouped with, we were the kids who, during tests, were trying to get the answers off other kids. Well, I started paying attention, I started studying, and I became a kid who was asked the answers. It happened during a test; a friend asked me to give an answer, and I said no. It caused a bit of drama at that time. Eventually, I got the most-improved-student award.

kelly **preston**

In high school, I went out for the boys' football team. I did it as a dare with my girlfriend Simone, and it turned into this whole fiasco. My girlfriend Simone and I, we would do these crazy things like wear my grandmother's muumuus to school with wigs, and tell people that it was an initiation ritual for a club and see what kind of reaction we would get.

Joining the football team was kind of a dare. I put my hair up in a baseball cap and actually made it through a couple of cuts. No one looked at me, but then I had to sign in and, well, I almost got expelled when the news came out. It was a very big deal.

kathy najimy

In junior high, I became an activist. There was a class for boys called Bachelor Survival where they learned how to cook,.clean, and do laundry. I remember thinking, Bachelor Survival *means men have to clean only when they're not married. After that women do it for them?* I was so angry. Here the girls had to take Home Ec, and they were taking Bachelor Survival! My friends and I, we drew up a petition to change the name of that class so that it would be Home Ec for Boys.

denyce graves

When I was in junior high school, there was a girl named Maria. She was a cheerleader, she was really cute, and all the guys liked her. She was so popular, everybody knew her in the school. She and her best girlfriend, Valerie, would come in to school every Monday talking about the great weekend they'd had.

They were always laughing; they were always whispering; they had secrets.

They were always laughing; they were always whispering; they had secrets. Maria was sort of the party girl. If you threw a party, you wanted her there. I remember one afternoon she said to me, "Do you want to go to the store with me?" I loved hanging out with her, so I said yeah. So we went to the store together to buy junk food.

And I will never forget this: She paid with food stamps. She said to me, "Just because you use food stamps doesn't mean you're poor."

"I know," I said. After all, I knew what food stamps were, because my family had them. In that moment I realized so much. The veil was lifted, the myth was shattered and she and I had our secret. I thought Maria was courageous. I realized then that people's struggles are not always so easy to detect.

anna quindlen

When I was in seventh grade—I can't even remember the circumstances—someone had done something bad and our teacher wanted us to say who had done it. She made me stand up in class and said that I had the obligation to tell. I think I might have been the class president that year; there was some reason why she picked me. But I refused. I felt that it was not an honorable thing to do, and I got in trouble, and I remember that almost physical sensation of standing there and thinking, *I don't care what happens, I can't do this.* It wasn't until later that I recognized it as a kind of courage.

sue grafton

when i was a girl...

I was afraid of everything. I was afraid of needles. I was afraid of an inchworm. I was afraid of other people. I thought other people were treacherous, particularly in elementary school, which I thought was a dangerous time in life. I remember sudden, inexplicable shifts in friendship; you'd go home for one day with a cold, come back, and everything would be different. I also tend to be now—and apparently I was then—a governed person. I never understood what the rules were, but I lived in terror of breaking them.

I never understood what the rules were, but I lived in terror of breaking them.

Reading seemed like a pretty safe activity, compared to the horror of the rest of it. I was fortunate that I grew up in a time with no television and no computers. I also happened to live in a neighborhood with a lot of children, so we invented game after game after game—I think that it allowed both my sister and me to develop imaginations.

I grew up in Louisville, Kentucky, and we lived in an old farmhouse that had once been part of a much larger piece of land. At the time we moved in 1940—which was the year I was born—the land had so shrunk, there was about a third of an acre left. There were many trees, many corners, nooks, and crannies to play in. The kids would assemble and create incredible dramas in which people got strung up the trees and tricycles got overturned. My friend Kathy and I once went through the neighborhood with our dollies nestled in beds of Kotex. I didn't know what a Kotex was, but it seemed like a really good mattress pad for a dolly. We also once found a bat that we put in this little basket. We covered it up and knocked on doors, asking people if they wanted blackberries. "Sure," they'd say. Then we'd open the basket and shriek. As fearful as I was, I did have my criminal streak then. It has to come from somewhere.

As fearful as I was, I did have my criminal streak then.

I remember going around the neighborhood with my sister—I must have been four or five, which means she was eight or nine—and the brothers Bobby and Don had decided to kill David Crass with a broom. I remember the incredible chase through the neighborhood. I was convinced the murder was going to happen and so I clung to my sister's hand, convinced that even murder was something she could save me from. In the end, they let him scamper off, but she took care of me. Though she could torment me. She was incredibly clever. If we did dishes together and I washed, she would dry, then she'd go, "Ha ha, I finished before you." So then I would have to beg, "I want to dry! I want to dry!" Or if I had to wash, she would go, "Eww, look at all those things floating around in the water!" She drove me stark raving mad, which is probably why I was a whiny child.

My family life changed when my father went into the army during World War II. I can almost divide my life into two parts: the first five years and then when my father was sta-

SUE GRAFTON

tioned in India. My mother was left in a large house alone with two young girls, and I think it was a tremendous burden for her. I understand that she wrote to him every day that he was gone, so I know there was a great deal of correspondence between the two. But when he came back, the family dynamic changed. Why that is, I do not know. In those days, I think, when the fellas came back from overseas, there was a spirit of such joy, and it took the form of a lot of whiskey drinking, a lot of smoking, and a lot of parties. I think my parents got caught up in that, and that was not necessarily good for their relationship.

> She had all manner of remedies: If you had nightmares, she would have you sleep upside down on the bed or turn your pillow over; in our childish minds, this seemed to do the trick quite nicely.

My mother was very pretty. She had a lot of energy and she was very well liked by people. She was the mother who chatted with everybody. Of course, this became a source of humiliation and embarrassment to me later in life. But she was a wonderful mother—par-

ticularly when I was not well. She had all manner of remedies: If you had nightmares, she
would have you sleep upside down on the bed
or turn your pillow over; in our childish minds,
this seemed to do the trick quite nicely. Also,
when I was sick, she would sit by my bed and
trace with her finger all the contours of my
face—it was incredibly restful. When you were
recovering, you got to eat milk toast—which
today seems pretty repugnant, but then
seemed quite lovely.

My sister and I were Daddy's little
girls. We adored him. When he was in the
army, he would send us stories. He had a fel-
low officer draw wonderful little pictures for
us, so we got to look forward to that. And
when he got back, he would whistle taps to us
before we went to sleep. He often sat with us
on the front steps and told us stories, and
some of them were so piteous that he would
weep himself. It certainly helped me to understand the notion of storytelling and the bonds
that can exist between parents and children.
They were simple stories, whether they were
read in a book or invented on the spot.

Ours was a family that read books and
talked about books. Summer evenings, we
would walk—the four of us—to the drugstore
and buy paperback novels for twenty-five
cents. My sister and I started with comic

SUE GRAFTON

books, which had a side benefit, of course. When the comic books got old, my sister and I would put them in a wagon and go around the neighborhood, selling them for two cents— thus profiting at the same time.

Summer evenings, we would walk— the four of us—to the drugstore and buy paperback novels for twenty-five cents.

My mother—to this day, I don't know how—had a revolving drugstore rack. She would read paperbacks, put them in this drug-store rack, and mark in pencil "dirty," "dull," or "good." My sister and I, as long as we were quiet, got to choose any book we wanted. My parents tended to favor mystery novels. The Mickey Spillane ones often said "dirty" on the cover, but we liked that. I think their reasoning was after we read enough of the dirty ones, we would realize that those were really the dull ones and then we should shift our taste over to the good.

i read

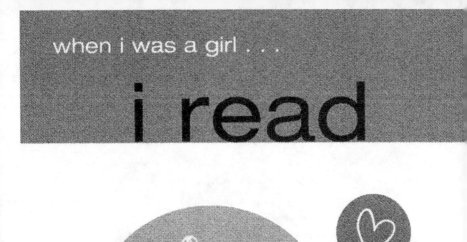

anna quindlen

When I was very small, I liked the Madeline books. She was the kind of kid I wanted to be, the kind who would say "Poo poo" to the tiger. It's a good lesson: If you are strong and you say "Poo poo" to the tiger, Ms. Clavel will grab you by the scruff of the neck, take you home, and you'll end up in the hospital with appendicitis.

> If I read a book that impresses me,
> I have to take myself firmly in hand
> before I mix with other people;
> otherwise they would think
> my mind rather queer.
>
> —Anne Frank

jean smart

The one book my dad would always read to us was *The Wind in the Willows*. I loved Toad and Mole and how they lived in those little houses on the river. Now I read that book to my son every night.

jane pratt

I loved *The Iliad* and *The Odyssey*. My dad would tell me the stories. We weren't allowed to hear the regular fairy tales, because they were sexist and racist.

We weren't allowed to hear the regular fairy tales, because they were sexist and racist.

So he would tell us the story of *The Iliad* and *The Odyssey*.

candice **bergen**

The House at Pooh Corner and *The Wind in the Willows* were my favorites.

dee dee myers

Harriet the Spy, I think I was in third grade when I read it. Harriet was this cool girl who lived in Manhattan and snooped around. I don't remember the plot so much as I remember the character. She was curious and independent, and slightly on the edge of mischief.

michelle **rodriguez**

As corny as it may sound, *Celestine Prophecies* was the book that made me feel like *Wow, you can actually read a whole book, Michelle. Celestine Prophecies* was the first book I actually finished, and that was at the age of sixteen.

marian wright edelman

When I was a girl, I read a lot of folklore. In fact, I have some of the ragged books in my house today. I look back at them and some of them are quite racist. I read *The Jungle Book* and Brer Rabbit—he was always so shrewd, how he could outtalk people.

teri garr

I liked to read Nancy Drews, but mainly I liked biographies. I wanted to see how stars became successful. I wanted to know the formula. But there never was a formula. Everybody did it a different way.

The Eighties

I WORE

Benetton sweaters
Combat boots
Rainbow barrettes
Monogrammed sweaters
Izods
Visors
Headbands
Bandannas
Parachute pants
Wispy bangs
Converse Hightops
Fair Isle sweaters
Alligator shoelaces
Reeboks
Doc Martens
Tretorns
Stan Smith Adidas
Rubber bracelets
Flashdance sweatshirts

I ATE/DRANK

Skor chocolate bars
Slim-Fast shakes
Nothing that wasn't on the
    Grapefruit Diet
Pasta
Designer jelly beans
Flavored popcorn
Rockadile Red Kool-Aid
Fro Yo
Mix In: ice cream

I DANCED

The Rock Lobster
The Time Warp
The dance from *Footloose*
The Moonwalk

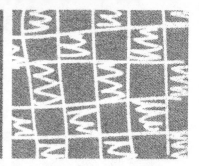

I WORSHIPED

Madonna
Michael Jackson
The Cast of *Dynasty*
Sylvester Stallone
Ricky Schroeder
Soleil Moon Frye
Tiffany
Debbie Gibson

> If I was a girl again, I would like to be like my fans, I would like to be like Madonna.
>
> —Madonna Ciccone

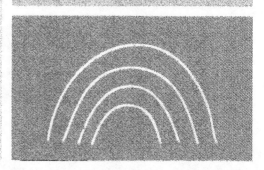

I WATCHED

My MTV!
The Cosby Show
The Facts of Life
The Breakfast Club
Diff'rent Strokes
Growing Pains
Who's the Boss?
Ferris Bueller's Day Off
Punky Brewster
Silver Spoons
The A-Team
Dirty Dancing
The Smurfs
Back to the Future
Sixteen Candles

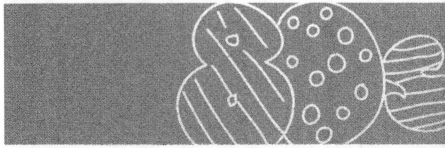

I LISTENED TO
The Cure
The Smiths
Bananarama
The Bangles
The Go Go's
The Talking Heads
Joy Division
New Kids on the Block

I READ
Judy Blume
Jackie Collins
Sassy magazine
The Fabulous Five by Betsy
  Haynes
Beverly Cleary

I USED
Anaïs Anaïs
Chanel Number 5
Black lipstick
Carmex
Sun-In

The Eighties

edie falco

when i was a girl . . .

I never felt like I looked right or behaved the right way or said the right things. I don't know if I thought of myself as a little girl—more as a little person. I knew I wasn't a boy, but I didn't fit in with the girls—they seemed pretty and dainty, not two words I would have used to describe myself. I grew up in the suburbs of Long Island, and I don't think I wore shoes the first fifteen years of my life. I was running around, climbing trees, and beating up neighborhood boys—bad stuff. Those were the days long before we were wearing watches. I never knew what time it was.

If I was most afraid of anything, it was other people. I had a terrible time of it. I was very awkward. I felt like all the other kids had gotten Cliff Notes on how to act. They knew how to be social and smart, and I didn't get it. I always got it wrong. I needed someone to tell me the rules, I was starved for someone to tell me the rules.

I needed someone to tell me the rules. I was starved for someone to tell me the rules.

I knew who was in the popular clique, but I hadn't the vaguest notion how to work my way into it or even if it was something I wanted. I always had the wrong type of sneakers and clothes. The bad dream kids all have? It actually happened to me. I went to school with my dress unbuttoned. A little kid named Eddie was the one to tell me. Very politely he said, "You might want to button the back of your dress." That was the kind of thing that happened to me—and only to me. At least that's how it felt: that I could never get it right.

I had my first best friend in elementary school; her name was Delphine. We used to sit at the piano and make up songs. She was beautiful, very, very popular, and so, so smart. All the boys had crushes on her. This was before I knew to be intimidated by girls like this. Later on, I would have steered clear of someone very popular and pretty, someone who got lots of attention.

So many times, I'd say something, and walk away thinking, *You are such an idiot.* Either I'd said the wrong thing, or used the wrong tone, or received a funny look from the person I said it to. I felt like a freak. Like I was built wrong. Like they forgot a part.

I felt like a freak. Like I was built wrong. Like they forgot a part.

My mother was the type of woman who made the rules up as she went along. And people, it seemed, changed the game according to my mother's rules. She would decide she was sick of the job she had, so she'd look in the paper, see an ad, think, *Well this seems interesting.* Then she'd spend the weekend learning how to do whatever the job called for. Then she'd get it. And she'd be the best.

My mother did community theater at night. In my opinion, life could get no cooler. *You have your daytime job and then you go out in the evening with other grown-ups who*

EDIE FALCO

say lines and act things out. I became one of
those little kids who go to plays all the time. I
went to her rehearsals and her performances.
I was maybe seven years old at the time and I
used to give her feedback. That she and her
friends were allowed to do this as grown-ups
was beyond crazy fantastic—I couldn't get
over it.

That she made this whole mish-mash-
conglomerate-of-a-life has affected everything
I've done since. She made it very clear that
there was nothing you couldn't do if you
wanted to do it. That was how she lived her
life, and that's what I learned from her.

She made it very clear
that there
was nothing you
couldn't do
if you wanted to do it.
That was how she
lived her life,
and that's what I learned
from her.

spotlight

I moved to a new town in the beginning of high school. I was so nervous about having to get new friends and having to fit in. I planned on sticking to my schoolwork, because I knew I could do that well. But eventually I joined the choir, and, for me, that was a turning point. The choir conductor, Mr. Velario, instilled in me the idea that singing beautiful music in front of people could potentially connect me to something bigger, to some other place. He taught me Brahms and Bach. He felt that if you were well trained, if you understood the music despite its being in a different language, you could transcend everything, be part of something larger. It was an introduction to spirituality, really, the idea that by lighting a flame, it might end up becoming a bonfire.

It was an introduction to spirituality, really, the idea that by lighting a flame, it might end up becoming a bonfire.

EDIE FALCO

When I was a girl, I just worried so much. Alone. With people. With family. With friends. There was a lot of worrying. Now I have a great deal of faith in things going the way they are supposed to. It was rough, feeling so traumatized all the time. I'd like to reach that little kid I once was, and tell her to take it easy.

I'd say to her, "You're a good kid. Don't worry so much."

me

To **moi**, beauty and
good breeding are,
like a pig and her frog,
inseparable.

—Miss Piggy, *Miss Piggy's Guide to Life*

the mirror

kathy najimy

I was mesmerized by myself.

I remember seeing myself in the mirror of Mother's dresser. I had lipstick all over my chin, and I think the comb got stuck in my hair. In my eyes, I was just beautiful. I was mesmerized by myself.

candace bushnell

I went through this really nerdy phase. I was into horseback riding, and all of the girls who rode horses always had dirty hair—and didn't care. I wore a dirty ponytail, and these cat's-eye glasses, which really weren't cool back then. My mother took me to this hair salon. I really wanted to have blond hair. I remember thinking, *Why can't they just come out with a pill that makes your hair come out of your head blond?* I got my hair cut really short and frosted, which was incredibly painful because they put that rubber cap on your head and pull out little bits of hair with a crochet needle. Oh, it was so painful! Later, I was up in our barn with my new short hair and my contact lenses, which I got around the same time, thinking I was looking very groovy. These huge farmer guys came to deliver the hay. I was standing up in the hayloft and this one guy looks up and yells, "Hey you! Hey you, boy! Get down here and give us a hand!"

I remember thinking, *Why can't they just come out with a pill that makes your hair come out of your head blond?*

In my own mind, I am still that fat brunette from Toledo, and I always will be.

—Gloria Steinem

lisa leslie

I don't remember being really critical of myself, or what I look like, until I was an adult. I don't think I was really in touch with myself in that way. When I looked in the mirror, the most important thing to me was that I was clean, that my hair was combed, and that my clothes matched. When I was playing basketball, I was very conscious of what colors I had on—if it was red shorts, I wanted to wear a red shirt and my socks had to have red in them. It was important for me to look presentable. I probably had a shape, but I didn't know it.

I don't think being taller than everyone else bothered me as much as it bothered me that people assumed I played sports *because* I was tall. I just thought it was rude that people who didn't know me would stop me on the street and ask me if I played basketball. That was bothersome to me—until I started playing basketball.

denyce graves

I used to sing into the mirror, using a hairbrush as a microphone. I was an outsider, so I had to come up with ways to entertain myself. When I looked into the mirror, I liked who I was. I mean, there were things I didn't like—my forehead, my nose. But I liked my mouth, lips, and teeth. And for the most part, I don't think I looked into the mirror and assaulted who I was. I looked in the mirror more for dialogue and entertainment.

When I looked into the mirror, I liked who I was.

sandra **bernhard**

When, as a teenager, I looked in the mirror, I saw someone who wasn't quite developed, who was a little awkward and extremely skinny. Had I been able to step into a time machine and go ahead fifteen to twenty years, I probably could have gotten a job as a model in

New York. But the timing sucked. I hadn't grown into myself yet. It was okay. I had a shaggy haircut and wore a lot of granny dresses.

There was this cowboy element in my high school. In the halls, kids would be, like, "Oh, look at her." "She is *so* skinny." "You are *so* ugly." They called me nigger lips and stuff like that. I was never really embarrassed by any of it. I think my perception of myself was totally rocking and exemplary. I knew where I was headed, so it was kind of, like, "Okay, well, I'll just get through this and have a couple laughs along the way."

melissa etheridge

The adolescent years were hard. I was coming into my body and sexuality, and my sexuality was confused. It was hard to look at myself and think, *Okay, I'm not like my pretty girlfriends who like to brush their hair and put clothes on, but I like my pretty girlfriends, so what's the deal?* So, it was very difficult to look in the mirror. I never quite got the clothes right. I never had the hair. I sort of just bumbled through.

lisa ling

When I was a little girl, I didn't like what I saw in the mirror because I didn't look like everyone else at elementary school. I had black hair and slanted eyes and it was very frustrating to look that way at that time.

jamie-lynn sigler

I used the mirror to perform, to run lines, to pretend I was playing a part. I don't think I ever looked at myself and thought I was beautiful. But I wasn't disappointed in what I saw either.

Not that I was vain or anything. I just loved it. I felt that the more I did, the prettier I could be.

I was always playing with makeup and hair stuff, experimenting and running through my mother's things. Whether I had rollers in my hair or I was curling my eyelashes, I loved playing in front of the mirror. Not that I was vain or anything. I just loved it. I felt that the more I did, the prettier I could be.

jane pratt

I always thought I was pretty, and I didn't find out,
until really late in the game, that I was sadly mistaken.
I grew up just totally assuming I was pretty, that my
friends were pretty—wasn't that great?—everybody
was pretty! Boarding school was a rude awakening.
There was a whole new standard for pretty. Here I'd
been thinking I was okay, and all of a sudden I had to
do something. Until then, looking in the mirror had
been fine.

michelle rodriguez

When I looked in the mirror, I saw a stick. I was like a
piece of clay that wasn't molded correctly. I didn't
stare in the mirror that much,
because I wasn't interested in
what I saw.

wendie malick

When I looked in the mirror, I saw someone skinny and scrawny. I really wanted to wear high heels, but didn't feel like I could because I was too tall. I also really wanted to be a cheerleader, but they all had calves and I didn't. I used to try to exercise them.

My nickname was Weed, a horrible nickname for a young girl.

I was one of the tallest kids in my school. The summer before I turned twelve, I grew two and a half inches, but none of it went horizontally. It was all vertical. My nickname was Weed, a horrible nickname for a young girl. I remember this one time all the girls were crying in the bathroom because our favorite teacher, the music teacher, was getting married and leaving. And everybody cried on my shoulder, because I was the tallest. All I wanted was to be the same size as they were, to be like everyone else. I didn't particularly like my body until I got older. I like it much more now than I did when I was a teenager.

susan lucci

When I was a little girl, I was very shy and I played in front of the mirror a lot. I made up stories and acted out all the parts and voices. I would sing and dance all over the house, and invariably, I would wind up in front of this one mirror in the upstairs bathroom that was next to a window with white curtains. I loved those curtains. They could make me a bride; they could make me an Arabian princess; they were my first communion kit. I was everything with those curtains.

ann curry

I was the fattest girl in third, fourth, and fifth grade. I was called *Blubber Lips, Fatty*. I was a chunk butt. It's funny: You can grow up and no longer be chunky and no longer be fat, but still feel, in your head, that you are. Sixth-grade summer, I swam every day, and, well, I grew up. When I came back to school, my friends didn't recognize me. Boys in sixth grade who I'd known in fifth grade asked me, "Are you a new girl?" I had no idea I had lost all my baby weight, but I was relieved not to be teased anymore.

I didn't like looking in the mirror. Men and boys started looking at me at the onset of puberty—maybe because I was tall—and I didn't want to be singled out. I started to wear big clothes. I tried to hide.

I was called *Blubber Lips, Fatty.* I was a chunk butt.

I remember once being in the pool—I think I was in sixth or seventh grade—and my father told this man he needed to stop playing ball with me, because I was a girl. And I was so shocked. I didn't realize what was happening, and then it hit me: Oh, oh! All of a sudden you're not a kid anymore. People want things from you that you don't understand.

I hated the idea of the attention. I didn't think I was pretty. You know why? Because everybody perceived to be pretty at that time was blonde! With curly hair and blue eyes! I was so not that. I had these big fat lips. People pay good money for these lips today, but back then they were considered ugly. My mother gave me some great advice. She said,

"Anna, beauty kinda funny, you know? You, everybody, gonna lose beauty. Everybody. But you never gonna lose this beauty in your heart." This is not to say that she didn't worry about my makeup or my hair or all that stuff. But she was letting me know that I better have something else going for me.

elizabeth perkins

When I looked in the mirror when I was a teen, what did I see? I saw someone who was very misunderstood. I saw a geeky girl, a farm girl in a red-and-white checked blouse and pigtails. I saw Elizabeth, who lives in this little farmhouse and shovels chicken manure, sells eggs by the side of the road, and takes the bus to school.

That image was hardly where I thought I should be. I thought that one day I would be Joan Crawford. I'd look in the mirror and think, *With the right wig, I'd look great.* I figured all I needed was a mink stole and maybe some diamonds.

 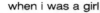

dee dee myers

When I was twelve--or maybe thirteen--I went to
summer school. I took a coed gymnastics class. I
don't know why everyone was getting on the scale--
maybe we had to determine our weight for spotting
or something?--but we all weighed ourselves. I was
103 pounds. Then, Mike Anderson got on the scale
and he weighed 102 pounds. I remember thinking, *Oh
my god! I'm taller and I'm bigger than all the guys.* It
was a horrifying thought. So back then, when I would
look in the mirror, I'd see this too-tall, goofy kind of
girl. Some girls seem to go through puberty so effort-
lessly. I didn't have a particularly large amount of
acne, but for me, every zit felt like a rebuke.

tanya tucker

When I looked in the mirror, I saw a little girl in pigtails, freckles, and a gap between her front teeth. I
had a brown stain on my front teeth and I was always
self-conscious of it. In front of the mirror--that's
where I stayed a lot of the time. I was singing songs
and the mirror was a teacher for me. It showed me
what other people saw.

my body

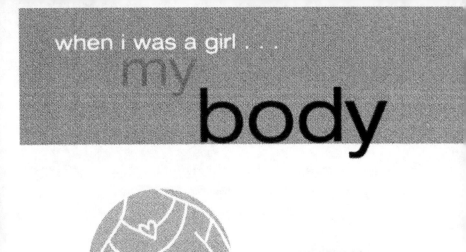

rita moreno

I asked for a bra when I was about seven. Latina girls usually develop early, and I bugged my mother so much she finally got me this tiny little thing like a postage stamp. I ran into the room to put it on. I looked in the mirror fully expecting to see breasts. I let out a howl that had my mother come running: "These are learners! I don't want learners!" I cried. I expected to see a fully developed bosom when I put it on.

If you're a Latina, you really owe yourself a pair of breasts.

At thirteen, I was still very skinny. I still had no chest, and I desperately wanted one. All girls do. But if you're a Latina, you really owe yourself a pair of breasts. Hips I had; breasts, I didn't. I started to wear padding, which terrified me. I was scared they'd come out in the public pool—as, one day, they did. I looked up from under the water, gasped, and almost drowned. Two big rubber falsies were floating over my head. Oh! Oh! Oh, god! I wanted to die.

sandra bernhard

I inquired about menstruation, and my mother sent away for a Kotex Starter Kit, which I adored. It had everything: the Kotex, the belts, and I thought that was just the coolest thing going.

Fashion is architecture:

It is a matter of proportions.

—Coco Chanel

anna quindlen

I was the flattest girl in the eighth grade. I remember once intercepting a note from one boy to another, saying that I was a carpenter's dream, flat as a board. For our first bras, my friend Donna and I went to a place called Bond's Department Store. You could walk there from our houses.

We bought Teen Form training bras, size triple A. They were completely and utterly flat, and I think they were $2.99. You had to wear one in eighth grade, whether you needed one or not. Clearly, I was in the *not* section.

illeana douglas

I grew up with boys. The last thing I would have wanted to think about was a bra. I left it to the last moment. This dance was approaching. I got my courage up at a department store and asked my mom about possibly getting a bra. She simply said, "Oh, you don't need one."

I thought, *Well, I guess that's the end of that discussion.* I went braless until I was thirty. No, not really. Maybe fifteen. I think I got one myself. I wasn't so keen on the idea.

kelly preston

I was a very slow developer. I had absolutely no breasts. I was every nickname in the book, from "Carpenter" to "Flat as a board." I desperately wanted to wear a bra. My parents let me get one— I was a sympathy case.

The other girls had breasts, but at least I had the line down the back. At least I had the bra strap.

Going to buy one was so exciting. It was a little triangle of nothing, but it was just fabulous and you could see it through shirts, tight T-shirts, especially. It made it okay. The other girls had breasts, but at least I had the line down the back. At least I had the bra strap.

sue grafton

Judy Joseph and I went down to Stewart's Department store and got fitted. My first bra was a double A with a tuck in it. We were really excited because what mattered in junior high school was having two straps.

If you were Southern, you did not *dare* let the sun shine through your dress.

We always had to wear a slip—if you were Southern, you did not *dare* let the sun shine through your dress—but girls who wore a bra *and* a slip showed great signs of advancement. The minute we got two straps, we knew we were okay.

alex kingston

I resolutely refused to wear a bra. In fact I don't think I wore a bra until I was twenty-two. I remember my mom going with me to a store, and the bras for juniors were so girly. They had little butterflies and flowers and sort of childish things on them. All the girls in school would wear them, but they didn't have anything to put in them. I didn't quite understand that. These girls had started shaving their legs and armpits, and my best friend and I resolutely weren't going to do any of that. We were going to be completely natural. And I was—until I was twenty-two!

ellen degeneres

I was raised Christian Science. I don't think we have hormones. My mother didn't even talk to me about my period. I remember when I got my period I was thirteen and I ran into the house singing, "This girl is a woman now."

jamie-lynn sigler

I was the last of my friends to get boobs, so it was a really depressing time for me. I remember being really upset about it and looking at my mom and my two grandmas. It was obvious something should have been coming. It was actually a really sensitive subject with me. It was eighth grade, it was really late, when I finally got them. We had to put shoulder pads in my bat-mitzvah dress to make me look like I had something.

India .Arie

I grew up in Denver, Colorado. Except for one other family, we were the only black people. I was the only black kid in my class; the only black kid in the neighborhood. But we had a good life. We always had a nice home with flowers in the front, grass in the backyard. We had bicycles and skateboards, Atari and television, video games, piano, pinball machine, TV, cable. We were spoiled. We didn't have anything to be afraid of, so we could just go outside and play. It was different back then. I used to ride my bike a lot. But more than anything, I was inside the house, playing an instrument or listening to records or singing.

My full name is India Arie Simpson. My birthday is the day before Gandhi's. Arie is my mom's middle name minus the M. I found out later on that in Hebrew *Arie* means lion. So when you think of Gandhi/peaceful and lion/aggressive, it makes for the duality I think I represent: masculine-feminine energy. I think

my name is my name for a reason. Even when
people make fun of it and call me India Jones,
I love my name.

I was a bad student. I never did my homework. I had a dirty locker too. My bag would be junky. I was junky.

My brother was always playing sports
and doing homework. I was the opposite: I
never did anything I didn't want to do. I was a
bad student. I never did my homework. I had
a dirty locker too. My bag would be junky. I
was junky. My brother is so left brain and
neat, and I am so right brain and free and
messy. We shared a room until I was twelve
and he was fourteen. Initially, we had bunk
beds. But then we took them apart and split
the room—his side would be clean
and my side would be dirty.

We used to fight over
the TV. Whoever turned it
on first had the TV for the
day. So one day, I turned off
the TV because it was a
Sunday and I didn't like sports
and the only thing that came on
good on Sunday was *Star Search*.

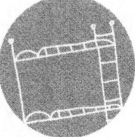

So I turned it off to wait for *Star Search* to come on. Well, my brother comes in, turns on his show, and acts like he'd been there first. Eventually, I got mad and threw a butter knife at him. Excepting that, we were the kind of family who always hugged and kissed each other. I'd say, "I love you, Mom," before I went out to play. Or my dad would pick me up and I'd grab his face and squeeze it real tight and kiss him to say, "Hey, Daddy!"

I got a lot of bad grades. In tenth grade I got grounded for two months. I had all D's and F's and one C on my report card. My mom actually didn't let me go downtown. That was shocking to me—we'd been grounded before; it was rare that we actually *stayed* grounded. As far as discipline went, I remember I used to cry and my daddy would say, "I'll give you something to cry about." Or I'd pout and he'd tell me to "Put that lip in."

My mom would say, "You know you are going to be written about someday, so watch how you live."

They were incredibly supportive. My parents would always say, "You know you can be anyone you want to be, right?" And from when I was ten, my mom would say, "You know you are going to be written about someday, so watch how you live." She was never a stage mother or anything like that, but she just knew.

I read spiritual stuff from a really young age. I remember reading astrology books and different articles about near-death experiences. We had this gigantic bookshelf with all kinds of yoga books and encyclopedias and records. When I was ten, I read stories about white light and people coming back from the dead. I learned about planets aligning and energy fields.

I think that when you are a kid, you just kind of react to the planet's energy without thinking about it: You are sad when it's gloomy outside, happy when it's sunny—you know, you just react to energy. I'm still like that. My friends will say, "India is such a brat. You can't be a little girl for the rest of your life." And I feel that, yes, I can. I can do whatever I want. I eat what I want. I wake up when I want to wake up. If I'm in a bad mood, I'm just in a bad mood—I don't care if I'm on TV in front of ten thousand people, one million people or what. I still feel like a girl in many ways.

lisa leslie

I loved the *Bionic Woman* and *Wonder Woman*. I thought the boots and the clear airplane were the best thing. I wanted to be the first black Wonder Woman. I also loved *Charlie's Angels*, because they wore swimsuits and were tough but feminine.

I wanted to be the first black Wonder Woman.

I loved those three strong and powerful women.

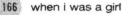

elizabeth Perkins

I spent most of my formative years on this very
remote farm in Southern Vermont, so I spent an
enormous amount of time in front of the television.
My early influences were Lucille Ball and Eve Arden.
My favorite character was Lily Munster on *The
Munsters*. She was doing that whole pre-Goth thing.
Seeing that in Hollywood you can dress up and be
whoever you want to be—I found that absolutely fas-
cinating. I was obsessed with Fred's big square head
and wondering how they made that. It was a fantasy
world and it drew me in.

cynthia nixon

I remember seeing the Vietnam War on TV, I remember that very much. I remember being very confused
by it. You turned on the TV and there was war, and
there were soldiers and people firing and people
being hit but when I walked out my door there was
no war there.

I remember Watergate on TV too. Because
my last name was Nixon, I always felt this tremendous simpatico with the president. I remember dis-
covering that my parents didn't like the president. I
couldn't understand. *He's the president, and my parents don't like him. Then how does he get to be the
president?*

kathy najimy

It's a new year and now I'm going to be a different girl.

I loved watching *Dick Clark's Rockin' New Year's Eve.*
I loved staying up late, but also it gave you the
chance to reinvent yourself. I remember feeling that
tomorrow would begin a whole new year. I'd think, *It's
a new year and now I'm going to be a different girl.*

lee ann womack

I was in high school when MTV started, and I remember turning it on and watching it and finding the
whole thing totally foreign. I didn't know any of the
artists; I didn't understand the music; it just didn't
mean anything to me. What I did notice? How it got
on my dad's nerves! So when he ticked me off, I
would go in there and turn on MTV.

denyce graves

I loved Angie Dickinson from the show *Police Woman*. I thought she was really, really cool and that was the first time I saw a woman as a cop. And I also loved Foxy Brown. She was a huge reason to celebrate—she was beautiful, she was strong, and she was dangerous.

jo dee messina

I remember watching *The Wonderful World of Disney* on Sunday nights. We'd pop corn and gather around the television. We'd be piled on the couch with blankets tossed over us, eating popped corn.

marian wright edelman

I used to love going to see Tarzan, but I always saw myself as Tarzan, not as Jane. I had a great fantasy life.

amy sedaris

I was a very happy child, pretty content.
There were six kids, my mom and my father.
At home everything was always a game.

We were all born in New York, but
when I was about four, we moved to North
Carolina. All our neighbors were Southern, so
it was kind of weird. We celebrated Greek holidays. Our Easter's about a week or two after
American Easter, so we were always outside
having Easter egg hunts when nobody else
was. It was just strange. My mom didn't cook
Southern food. We didn't speak with a
Southern accent. We were like the family on
The Munsters.

My father's mother, our grandmother,
lived with us for a while. She didn't speak any
English. She was all Greek and she was freaky.
She had long hair, which she wore in braids.
She arrived from New York with these big
containers of change from her shoe-shining
store in New York. She gave us a quarter for

doing something as simple as opening a door, and for that we loved her.

People would always say, "You're gonna be on *Laugh-In*." I always did stuff to try to get a laugh. But I never thought of myself, like, *Oh, I'm funny.*

My mother was at home all the time, which was nice. She was there when we woke up and when we got home from school. So we always had someone to tell our stories to. She was really pretty and had this great sense of style. She was always in the kitchen, always cooking. We all cook in my family—but that came from my mom. I loved grocery shopping. I went every Friday night with my dad. He taught me: If you dig in the very back in the shelf, you can find the cans the store clerks were too lazy to put the price tags on. So if you reach in the back, you get the old prices. He taught me shifty ways to shop. But I'm not a thrifty shopper. Living in New York, I'll go to five different stores to get what I want, but I don't care how much it costs. Like, I don't look for a bargain.

He taught me: If you dig in the very back in the shelf, you can find the cans the store clerks were too lazy to put the price tags on.

My mother was really, really funny, just goofy, and she was a real good storyteller. You could tell she would work the story. The first time you heard a story, it would be really funny. But, the sixth or seventh time she told it, it was edited, reworked. My brother David's a writer. I think he got that from her.

My mom made all our clothes, and I just loved going to the fabric stores and picking out the fabric. I had this lime green wet-look jumper. If you spilled something on it, it would just fall off. I loved that. And I was in Girl Scouts, so I was always in the uniform. I still love uniforms. If I get a job and it requires a uniform, I just love it. I've saved them all. Waitress uniform, security guard uniform, cop uniform, you name it; I just can't get enough of a uniform.

I was obsessed with shoes. Every day after school I would come home and put on my mom's high heel shoes. Then I'd go in my bedroom and do my homework. But the only way I could do my homework was if I pretended I had my own classroom and I was the

AMY SEDARIS

teacher. I would do my homework on this giant blackboard in my room. In my mind, I was teaching my homework to my thirty-two students. They all had names, and I gave them all report cards. I was a very mean teacher.

I played dress-up a lot. I started collecting wigs around third grade when my mom gave me my first fall. I'd look in the mirror and do character development. There was this little girl, she was from Costa Rica, and she was my best friend. I was obsessed with her mom. She had really messy hair and was kind of unattractive and sloppy. But whenever she had to go out, she was spectacular. It was like she was two different people. I remember being obsessed with her for that reason.

My mom wanted me to be a cop. She thought I'd be a good cop.

People would always say, "You're gonna be on *Laugh-In*." I always did stuff to try to get a laugh. But I never thought of myself, like, *Oh, I'm funny.* I liked funny things. I remember rolling around on the living room floor with my mom once thinking, *What am I gonna do when I grow up?* We tried to figure out what I could do. My mom wanted me to be a cop. She thought I'd be a good cop.

i wore

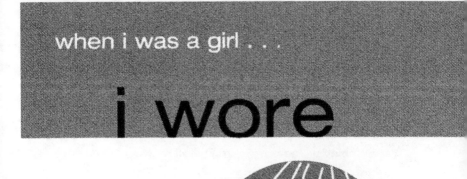

anna quindlen

I had this red dress that had three blackboards on the skirt. My mother took some sort of magical white paint and wrote on the blackboards: "My name is Anna. My daddy's name is Bob. My mommy's name is Pru." I thought that was the coolest dress in the whole world. I would swan around in this dress like nobody's business. I remember how heartbroken I was when it became clear that no matter how I sucked it up, I was no longer going to be able to button that dress anymore.

I would swan around in this dress like nobody's business.

> I base my fashion taste on what doesn't **itch.**
>
> **—Gilda Radner**

ellen **burstyn**

My mother made all my clothes—not the ones I wore to school, but my special clothes. She made me a lime-colored, almost chartreuse dress with lace sleeves and brown velvet ribbon running through it. It had bows and the skirt puffed out. I thought it was really Shirley Temple. Then she made me a rose-colored velvet jumper with straps that had inverted flowers on it. It went with a white satin peasant shirt. I thought that was pretty spectacular.

candice **bergen**

I had a pair of gold sandals that used to send me into reveries of delirium. I was maybe four or five, and I would walk around looking at my feet all the time. I was just insane for my gold sandals.

alex kingston

In England we have this modeling clay called
Plasticine that came in very bright colors. If you
could get all the Plasticine colors together and mush
them up, you would have these strands of gorgeous
color. I had this dress, it was kind of psychedelic,
and it looked like Plasticine: orange, yellow, and red.
It was a summer dress, sheer, with cotton underneath. Even when I was too big for it, I tried to
squeeze back into it.

jean smart

I had straight hair as a girl, and I was always jealous
of those girls who had wavy hair. My hair is baby fine,
and my mother would give me the most awful perms.
It was the bane of her existence. The perms would
smell, and they'd last only about a week, and she
would just be beside herself. She even permed my
bangs once. I have the picture—curled hair and
permed bangs. I was in the fifth grade, and oh, my
god, it was not pretty.

My favorite beauty product was Sun-In. If we
didn't have sun, we'd put it in our hair then heat it
with a blow dryer. Sun-In and frosted lipstick—those
were my favorites.

ann curry

We didn't have very nice clothes in my family,
because we didn't have a lot of money, so I don't
remember anything that I wore except this chocolate
brown dress. My mother made it for me, and it was
so pretty. It had a string of rhinestones around the
neckline and cuffs, and I wore it every chance I got. I
wore it for all my parties, for my birthday; I wore that
dress until it fell off of me, until there were transpar-
ent patches in the velvet. I wore it not just because it
was so pretty and velvety, but because she made it
and I knew how hard it was for her to find the time.

I wore that dress until it fell off of me, until there were transparent patches in the velvet.

This is the most ridiculous thing you'll ever
hear, but in high school my mother was actually hem-
ming up my skirts. And I would rip the hems out so
they would be longer. My mom wanted me so much
to be like every other American girl. She didn't want
me to suffer racism, or a feeling of being separate
from my culture. But to me it didn't matter so much. I
just wanted to be the smartest, the strongest, the
most awesome girl; I wanted to be the "hear-me-roar-
chick." When I ripped out the hems of my skirt, my
mom would go and hem them right back up, and
there I'd be, tugging at my skirt again.

sandra bernhard

When I was a girl, my favorite outfit had to be Danskins. They were always comfortable and chic.

denyce graves

I was watching *American Bandstand*, and these girls had white Go Go boots. I thought they were just so supercool. I asked for them for Christmas, and I'll never forget how happy I was to get them.

gillian anderson

When I was about fourteen, I found fashion. We went to London, and I came back with a little purple miniskirt and red leather shoes, a pink sweatshirt, and a streak of red in my hair. It was the '80s, and all of a sudden I felt I could express myself in another way. I enjoyed walking down the street and having people turn and stare. It was a means of self-expression and it appealed to the anarchy I felt at the time.

kelly preston

My mom made this one great yellow dress that had a little yellow fringe at the bottom. It was very simple, but because she made it, I loved it. Then I ran into a wall and got blood all over me and ruined it.

illeana douglas

I was around eight years old when I got into clothes. I had a blue velvet jumper and a red velvet jumper, and those were sort of my two favorite things. Then there was my Groucho Marx sweater, which my mother couldn't get off of me for all of high school. I had this white sweater with stripes on it, and Groucho Marx knitted in. (When I was fourteen or fifteen I discovered Groucho Marx and I became obsessed with him.) So that was my favorite sweater. My mom says it was a tie between that and my *Blazing Saddles* T-shirt.

jane kaczmarek

I lived in Wisconsin. The school board had a rule that girls couldn't wear pants to school. It was cold and people used to wear such short skirts. The rule of thumb—no pun intended—was that when you stood up, your skirt had to break right where your hand bent. If you try that now, it means the skirt would barely cover your heinie. So skinny legs were very important.

You couldn't buy worn-out blue jeans; you had to age them yourself. We had to rub our rear ends on the sidewalk to break down the denim.

I graduated from high school in 1974, and in 1972 they finally let us wear pants. Blue jeans were big possessions of coolness. Those years were big for Crosby, Stills, Nash, and Young. It was kind of that back-to-nature hippie time. You couldn't buy worn-out blue jeans; you had to age them yourself. We had to rub our rear ends on the sidewalk to break down the denim. Then you would wait until you had holes and patch them.

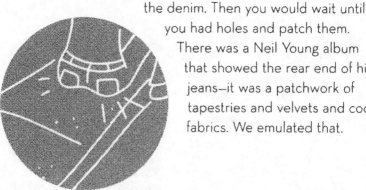

There was a Neil Young album that showed the rear end of his jeans—it was a patchwork of tapestries and velvets and cool fabrics. We emulated that.

fionnula flanagan

My favorite outfit was anything that *wasn't* my school
uniform. I think my favorite thing was a dress that was
sent to me from America. I had an aunt who lived in
Connecticut and she sent me this dress that was
pink gingham. It was so beautiful, I didn't want to
wear it. I just wanted to hang it up and look at it and
fantasize about wearing it. To this day, I can see it so
vividly. It probably had puffy sleeves and lots of lace
on the front; it probably came from a Butterfield pattern book. To me, it was very American.

rita moreno

My mother sewed and embroidered. When I was a
tiny girl, she made me pinafores with very ruffly ruffles on either side. I always felt like a little butterfly. I
used to go round the room flapping these ruffles
because they were so pretty.

I always felt like a little butterfly.
I used to go round the room flapping
these ruffles because
they were so pretty.

edie falco

My grandmother was a seamstress—still is and always was. She made matching coats and hats from plush-stuffed-animal kind of fur for me and my cousins. Any day I got to put them on, that coat and hat were perfect.

cynthia nixon

I had a fur poncho with llamas on it and a big fur collar that I really loved. And I had a red-and-white bikini with buttons and a little skirt. I would wear tutus around the house.

india.arie

I always loved jewelry and gems and crystals. When I was about ten, my dad bought me a turquoise ring. It broke, and then I linked it onto a bracelet, and then it fell off my bracelet. So on my fourteenth birthday, my dad decided I was old enough to have a real ring. My parents were divorced at this point, and he sent me a sapphire-and-diamond ring and a bracelet with rubies and diamonds going around it. I had the ring for a while, but I got eczema on my fingers and they swelled up and I had to cut the ring off. I kept it in a pouch for a long time, and then my senior year in high school, I lost the pouch. I was devastated.

elizabeth perkins

I had a pair of purple-and-white-checked bell-bottom hip huggers. I thought they were so attractive. I would wear them with this wide brown suede belt that had all these little holes in it. I just thought I was the coolest thing on the planet. I look back on those pictures now, and actually they're in style again. That's how much older I am now. In that outfit, I just thought I was so beyond suburban life. They had been sent to me by my father's girlfriend from New York City, so they were special, they were hip. They transformed me into a *Mod Squad* girl. I was Peggy Lipton! I wore those pants every day. Almost all of the pictures of me from that time, I'm wearing my purple-and-white bell-bottom hip huggers.

cherry jones

I had a routine. On Friday nights, after being tucked in, I'd jump out of bed and change into a pair of patterned pretty dungarees and a T-shirt. I had these great Keds. They were early '60s Keds with a pattern and they came up over the ankle. So every Friday night, I would put everything on—including my shoes—and get back in bed. This way, the minute I woke up on Saturday morning, I was ready to get out of the house and into the trees. Oh man, I loved those Saturday morning play clothes.

melissa
etheridge

when i was a girl...

I don't remember the first album I bought, but I remember the first one I received. For Christmas, my father got me Carole King's *Tapestry*. I'd listen to that backward and forward every day, five or ten times a day, just over and over. I'm so glad that that was the first album I latched on to, because she's just the perfect songwriter and those songs were just perfect pop songs.

Bless my parents' hearts, I don't have a memory of them saying, "Turn that down." My father, being a genius, like all dads in the '70s, put carpeting down in the basement, and we could go down there and listen to anything and close the door. I listened to everything from Led Zeppelin to Jackson 5 to The Who's *Tommy*. Also the London Symphony Orchestra version of *Tommy*.

My first concert was either The Eagles, Bad Company, or Peter Frampton. My girlfriends and I, we sat on the side of the stage and I remember there being a funny smell, and this was probably ninth or tenth grade. My dad, bless his heart, he was the dad who would drive us to Kansas City if we had to see the shows. It was, like, an hour drive, he would go do something—I don't know what—and then he would come back and pick us up. We never had that experience of hanging out with the weirdos. I went to concerts and got home safely.

In high school, I went to see A Star Is Born with Barbra Streisand and, Christ, I wanted that hair.

In high school, I went to see A Star Is Born with Barbra Streisand and, Christ, I wanted that hair. She went through a big fur thing in the late '70s too. I loved the way she looked. I went down to my local hair salon and said, "Give me a perm." I didn't get the beautiful long fur, but I got the horrible perm.

I was already on the music train when I was in high school. I was playing in bands, and I was listening to these songs, thinking about which ones would work for me. I didn't have that rebellious "Yo, Mom and Dad don't like this kind of music, so I'm gonna listen to it" attitude. I mean, my mother didn't like my radio stations, and in the car we'd listen to classical music, which was a bummer. But that was about it. They'd never put down my rock and roll music or my funk music.

I was the girl with the guitar and that was my identity.

Being musical was pretty much my identity in high school. If you ask any of my old classmates, they'll say, "'Miss'"—they used to call me that back then—"used to walk through the hallways with her guitar." I was the girl with the guitar and that was my identity. I sang in choir. I would have been in band, except I couldn't take that many music courses, so I had to drop out. But I sang all the time for my friends.

I was in the band at our junior prom. We had to play *Night Fever* by the Bee Gees over and over again. And I was in all the musicals—that was my identity in high school: music.

I was a huge Bruce Springsteen fan, but did I lust after him? No. I wanted to *be* him.

MELISSA ETHERIDGE

I didn't do the music idol thing in high school, because I was making music; I was standing up and doing it; I was listening and learning, so I never put anybody's poster up. I was a huge Bruce Springsteen fan, but did I lust after him? No. I wanted to *be* him. I wouldn't have been conscious in high school of lusting after a female because I was very confused in high school.

Growing up in the Midwest, in the '70s . . . I had boyfriends, I had friends, I was fine, but my heart wasn't there. Not knowing if I was a weirdo, why I was feeling the way I was, that was my heartbreak. Making music and writing music soothed me. I would put all of the questions, the wants, the desire, and the pains into the music. And I would write and play for hours.

edie falco

Joni Mitchell's songs feel like the soundtrack of my life. She feels like my own personal inner voice. I don't know if I could ever see her in concert, because I almost feel like I am her, that we've been the same person for a lot of years, and that she has a huge influence over me.

lee ann womack

I grew up in a little bitty town in East Texas, Jacksonville, population twelve thousand. It was a two-Dairy Queen town. That's what I call it. There's a Dairy Queen as you come into town and there's a Dairy Queen as you drive out of town. In fact, that's almost the only restaurant they have there.

    I grew up in a house that my grandfather built. It's the same house my mother grew up in, a farmhouse with a creek in the back. We had horses growing up; we had a dog, several cats, even some ducks at one time.

My mom played the piano really well, and she played a lot of Baptist hymns. So that's how I learned to sing harmony—standing on the pew next to her at church. I had to take piano lessons and I hated it. Now I'm glad I did it, but my mom could be very strict with me. She made sure we had a piano in the house even though they were expensive and she had us take lessons, which were not cheap.

I guess I spent my life in somewhat of a Walter Mitty-type existence. I just sat around and day-dreamed a lot. The truth is I always wanted to be a country singer. For as long as I can remember I wanted to go to Nashville and make records there, and so I spent my days in Jacksonville daydreaming. I watched the awards shows; I watched *Hee Haw*; I listened to the radio; I bought lots of albums and memorized the backs of them—who played what and who produced what and who the management company was.

When I was sixteen, I loved Vince Gill records. There was *Victim of Life* and *Turn Me Loose*. I would hear him singing and think, *How did he do that?* I'd rewind, listen to him again, and then I'd rewind, listen, rewind, rewind, rewind.

I guess you could say I educated myself on Nashville before I got to Nashville.

Music was **my refuge**.
I could crawl into the space between the notes
and curl my back to **loneliness**.

—Maya Angelou

illeana douglas

When I was a girl the happiest day of my childhood was Earth Day. My father had a band called Forty Acres and a Mule, and one day they discovered that I knew all the words to the Rolling Stones song "Angie." I was seven. The crowd was, like, "Who is this seven-year-old imitating Mick Jagger?" Then we drove home, listening to the Beatles sing "The Long and Winding Road." It was the groovy '70s, and that was probably one of the happiest days of my childhood.

tanya tucker

I had a dream of being a singer, and my dad gave up his life to try and help me chase it. Our first move for my career was from Wilcox, Arizona, to Phoenix. I went for a children's talent show that came on early in the morning. I became a regular on the show, singing songs like "How much is that doggy in the window" and "Here comes Peter Cottontail."

Here I'd been used to singing "Woman of the world leave my world alone," so it was quite a shock. Eighteen weeks into it, my dad said he couldn't take it anymore. So, we moved again and again, ending up in Henderson, Nevada, which is right outside of Las Vegas. By the time I was nine, we were living in Nashville, and I was attacking country music full throttle.

My relatives thought he was nuts, moving around for me. Looking back on it, he might actually have been crazy. How much he did for me, it baffles me.

If I had to pick a song that represented how I felt as a girl, well, I'd probably end up picking two songs. First, I'd pick "Daddy and Home," which is a Jimmy Rogers song about growing up and coming back to home. And the next would be "My Cowboy's Getting Old," a song I did on my first album. I was seventeen, and it's about how my dad was getting older and not being able to kick butt like he used to.

jo **dee** messina

I spent a lot of time at the roller skating rink, so I was exposed to disco and that funky town. My sister was a big Tom Petty fan, my older sister was a big Donny Osmond fan, and my brother was really into the Styx, Queen, and Rush. For my generation, it was Rick Springfield and Michael Jackson.

The Nineties

I WORE

Flannel shirts
Ripped jeans
Old T-shirts
Gap khakis
Doc Martens
Slap bracelets
Striped leggings
Sunflowers
Long floral-print skirts
Rollneck sweaters

I ATE/DRANK

Gatorade Gum
Crystal Pepsi
Kid Cuisine TV dinners
Snapple
Arizona Iced Tea
Atomic Fireballs
Evian

I DANCED

The Lambada
   (the forbidden dance)
The Macarena
The Achy Breaky Heart
The Electric Slide

I WORSHIPED

Kerrie Strugg
Leonardo DiCaprio
Jared Leto
Mia Hamm
Kurt Cobain
Sharon Stone
Christian Slater
Madonna
Brad Pitt

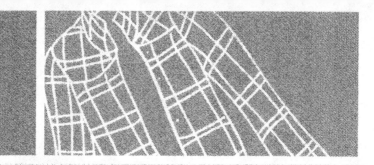

The hardest thing about moving forward is not looking back.

—Felicity Porter,

Felicity

I WATCHED
Beverly Hills, 90210
Seinfeld
Beavis and Butthead
TGIF
Party of Five
The Real World
The Simpsons
South Park
My So-Called Life
Titanic
Jurassic Park
Friends
Terminator 2
Buffy the Vampire Slayer
Felicity

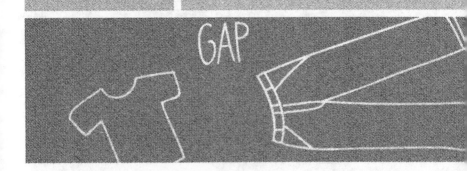

I LISTENED TO

Greenday
Nirvana
Offspring
Soundgarden
Pearl Jam
Phish
Lenny Kravitz

I READ

Christopher Pike
The Babysitter's Club
Sweet Valley High
R. L. Stine
Seventeen magazine
YM magazine
Cosmopolitan magazine

I USED

Baby Soft
Lip Smackers (with sparkles)
Eternity
CK1

The
Nineties

jane pratt

when i was a girl...

I went out on a limb and gave the cutest guy in my class a valentine. He had long blond hair and oh, my god! I had such a crush on him. I was twelve. I'll never forget the crush feeling. I wanted to smell him. I wanted to kiss him. I always was the first one to go for the kiss, always.

We went to see the movie *Fiddler on the Roof,* and I put my arm around him and kissed him. What was I thinking? I was the girl! Then I gave him Bob Dylan's *Greatest Hits* for Valentine's Day. I was really embarrassed because I guess it was just too much; I'd gone too far.

We went to see the movie
Fiddler on the Roof,
and I put my arm around him
and kissed him. What was
I thinking? I was the girl!

I was getting rejected constantly, I think because I was the aggressor. I had a boyfriend named Richie when I was thirteen. He went away for the summer, and we wrote the whole time. One letter had RG+JP on it, but it was all crossed out. I didn't realize it was crossed out, or I didn't recognize it as crossed out. I thought he was being artistic. I was all excited, so I sent him one back that had JP+RG and kisses on it, only to find out he'd meant it was over.

My mom always encouraged me not to feel like I needed a boyfriend. I remember her praising me to the skies because I was the only girl in junior high who didn't have a boyfriend. My mom was, like, "That is so cool that you are fine with yourself. You are good being independent. You are doing your own thing. Look how much you are getting done." That was the big thing: accomplishment. But when I did have crushes, I absolutely pursued them. I don't think I ever went out with a guy who pursued me. It was not about that. It was about me picking who I wanted; it was about the chase; it was about getting him. I wasn't good at first, but I got good after a while.

I actually remember wondering at a very young age if I was gay. My parents had a lot of gay and bisexual friends, we were very open, and I remember it was a topic of conversation among my friends.

"Do you think she is gay or straight?"

"Which way do you think Amy is going to go?"

"What about Ben?"

I remember being seven and riding my bike over to my friend's house and seeing this girl coming out of her house; she was probably a teenager. She looked like the perfect contestant on a dating game show. She had ashy blond hair, parted in the middle, straight down. She wore a minidress; she had frosty pink lipstick; she wore boots, probably similar to the boots I wear today, and I just thought, *Wow! That's beautiful.* It took me a couple more years to develop a sense of what was beautiful in a man. At first, my friends and I liked men with long hair and that smaller boned, more feminine look. But when I was twelve, and I got that crush, I was, like, "Oh no, sorry Mom, not gay."

I never had a fantasy about my wedding day. Ever.

I never had a fantasy about my wedding day. Ever. Recently, I was sitting with a friend at a wedding and she commented, "We've all dreamed about this since we were three years old." At that moment, I felt like the big outsider. I thought, *I have never had a fantasy about being married. I have never thought that being married is better than not being married.* I remember thinking even as a kid, *Well, it's not necessarily better for a man to be married, so why is it better for a woman to be married? We make money too.* I didn't understand. My mom says that when I was a little girl, I would say, "If I ever get married I want my husband to live in Europe." I didn't really comprehend what Europe was, what that meant. I guess I knew it was somewhere far away, and if my husband was there, I could still be independent and have my own life.

My mom was married three times, but we were not led to believe that being married was somehow an accomplishment. You either were or you weren't. I remember my mom being very proud of herself after getting divorced. She was proud to be making her own life and raising us basically on her own. As a girl, I probably had fantasies about getting divorced more than getting married. Divorce seemed like an accomplishment, but getting married seemed like the easy way out.

growing

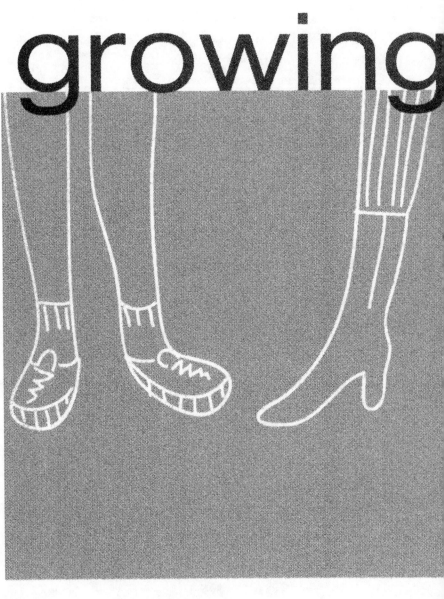

up

From the moment I was six
I felt sexy.
And let me tell you
it was hell, sheer hell,
waiting to do something
about it.

—Bette Davis

love

cynthia nixon

I hung out in a group of kids. There were twelve of us: eight girls and four boys. At my high school there wasn't this complete separation of the sexes. You were friends, you hung out, you talked. If you wanted to go out with someone, then it got formal. You'd say, "Would. You. Like. To. Go. Out. With. Me?" And the person would answer "Yes" or "No." Then, you would walk around with your arms around each other, and go and make out places. You were a couple until you got sick of each other, and then you would break up.

You'd say, "Would. You. Like. To. Go. Out. With. Me?" And the person would answer "Yes" or "No."

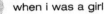

If Jordan Catalano is nearby,
my whole body knows it.
Like one of those dogs that point.
I'll keep talking and stuff, but my mind
won't even know
what I'm saying.
I keep wondering if there's
a term for this.

—Angela Chase, *My So-Called Life*

No one told me about the birds and the bees. I figured it out. My mother took me to see a play called *Spring Awakening* about all these teenagers at the turn of the twentieth century finding out about their sexuality, and there was a fair amount of stuff in there. I remember thinking, *Oh, okay* . . . And then I read *Forever* by Judy Blume, and that was kind of it.

elizabeth perkins

I knew that I had power over boys when I realized I didn't need them, when I realized that how I felt about myself was not going to be defined by whether the cute guy in the class liked me. I knew that I was never going to have to rely on a man to provide a life for me or teach me how to do everything. With that realization comes a power.

jean smart

My first really big, big crush was at summer school. It was music summer school. I played the cello and there was this boy, Sandy, who played the drums. He was always getting in trouble because he would do things to try to make me laugh.

Anyway, he carried my cello home a few times— no easy feat!—and I thought he was adorable. I went to his house one day. We were hanging out in the basement, and he tried to kiss me. I wouldn't do it. I was eleven at the time.

I remember not saying anything to my mother about it, but then one night—toward the end of summer school—she found me crying and crying and crying into my pillow because I was going to miss him so much. I would never cry in front of anyone, but I was so devastated. I think that's one of the reasons I became an actress, so I could get paid to cry in front of people—because, it's not easy for me.

joan chen

When I was a girl I didn't kiss anybody.

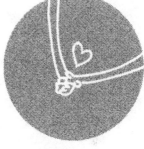

When I was a girl, romantic love was forbidden among the youth. It wasn't talked about, but that doesn't mean it wasn't felt. Today I think high school students in Shanghai might feel okay with holding hands, even kissing. But I didn't kiss a boy until I was twenty—and that was after I knew I would be coming to America. So really, when I was a girl, I didn't kiss anybody.

lisa leslie

I remember in third grade, I told my mom, "I don't want to be friends with Gail anymore, because she lets the boys hump her." In my opinion, that was the worst thing that could happen: You'd let the boys look under your skirt. I used to wear a skirt with shorts underneath, because I twirled on the bars and I never wanted a boy to see up under my skirt. She did that, and I didn't want to be her friend anymore.

I knew I had power over boys when I started getting picked first for kickball.

I knew I had power over boys when I started getting picked first for kickball. That started happening in fourth grade P.E. and it was a sign, because usually a boy would pick all the girls last.

candace bushnell

My father didn't want any of us to have boyfriends, which didn't matter because I wasn't that interested in them. I think I made out with a boy when I was fifteen or sixteen, but I thought it was really slobbery. I think I kind of had a boyfriend, because there was this guy—I'd go to his house occasionally and we'd make out. He had all these older brothers and we would go to the basement, and they'd be there listening to The Who. I guess he was sort of like a boyfriend, but I never really talked to him in school. He did make me this box in wood shop, which I'm pretty sure I still have in my parents' house. It was very sweet.

jane kaczmarek

I remember sitting in a health class in high school. We were supposed to go around and say what we were attracted to in boys, you know. Almost everyone in my class said, "Cars." And I remember saying, "Good verbal skills." I just loved people who talked. I still do. I had a wonderful boyfriend from the next school over. His name was Park Orchard, and he was a good guitar player, a good singer, and very, very funny.

> **I remember walking down the stairs and having my mother say, "You march right on upstairs and put on a bra."**

Park and I went to the prom together. The theme was *Stairway to Heaven*. I wore a green sweater dress. I remember walking down the stairs and having my mother say, "You march right on upstairs and put on a bra." And I put a bra on under the dress, then quickly took it off and left it in the glove compartment of my friend's car. It was just for a fashion choice, not for anything sexual. Meanwhile, Park wore a fetching powder blue, elephant bell tuxedo with a monster bow tie and ruffles; he wore his hair down to his shoulders and big platform shoes. He looked ridiculous, but I thought he was really cool. I think I voted for myself for prom queen. They posted the results, and there was only one vote after my name. (I'm glad I'm reminding anyone who went to Greendale High School of that!)

It's shocking, the level and the depth I felt at that age.

I had another boyfriend named Rusty Long. I was so enamored the brief period he smiled on me. Rusty had very shaggy hair, he was a good tennis player, and all the girls liked him.

Recently, I was home, and I found a bunch of poems and letters we'd written one another. It's shocking, the level and the depth I felt at that age. To find this cache of written declarations, of love was so deep. There was this Linda Ronstadt song we used to listen to together, and I heard it the other day and it just knocked me off my pants. It was a song that made me realize he'd never feel about me the way I felt about him.

sue grafton

I fell in love for the first time in kindergarten. His name was Nelson, and we sat across from each other and kicked feet, and took our little naps together on the rug. Then there was George. Grade by grade, I was in love with somebody else. My first big crushes were on movie actors. Stewart Granger was as close to perfection as I could imagine. He was aristocratic, very patrician-looking, handsome but with a smooth face, and good cheekbones. I thought he was just fabulous. Robert Taylor was another one, but these are actors you hardly ever hear of anymore.

I always had a boyfriend or a steady or something like that. I was part of a school youth group, so we tended to be a little pristine—there was nothing much down and dirty going on. We were all committed to the church. Once our youth group had somebody come to discuss sex with us. We got to write down questions on pieces of paper, and on one of those pieces of paper was "What if you get sperm in your underpants?" I thought that was an outrageous question. I knew someone in that group was pretty worried about sperm. It gave me a little hint that stuff I didn't know about was going on.

I was in the sixth grade and a kid used the work f-u-c-k, and I didn't know what that was. "Well, go ask your daddy," the kids said to me. I did and I am not sure I got a straight answer. This girl Cheety, her parents had some sex objects in a little cigarette box. It was like getting a glimpse of life's torrid possibilities, but in sixth grade I wasn't so interested.

gladys knight

when i was a girl …

My brother and I would play piano until we heard this voice come in from the kitchen where my mom and aunts were. "Stop that banging!" they'd scream. We used to bang, bang, bang. That was when I was two years old and I see my whole life from that time on.

We lived in Atlanta in my aunt and uncle's apartment. There were six of us in my immediate family. My sister Brenda was sort of like a bookworm. She was very smart and she was the first one in our family to go to college. My brother Baba was always a comedian. He used to keep us in stitches. He loved to sing, but he couldn't dance a lick. And my baby brother, David—he became like a son to me, so to speak.

My mom would make this oatmeal.
It wasn't the thick kind because we
didn't have a whole lot and she had
four kids to feed. So she made it
very thin and poured it in a jar with
butter, milk, and sugar.
We would drink it hot, snuggled
down between those sheets.

You know the saying "It takes a village to raise a child?" That's how it was for us. My grandmother and my aunt lived with us in the very early stages of our childhood. We had dinner together every night. We had to do our homework at specific times. My parents would tuck us in at night. It sounds like a storybook, doesn't it? But sometimes we had hard times where maybe the electricity was off. I never liked the dark. Even the candles scared me. If the heat had been turned off, I remember my mom and dad would come and stay with us. My mom would make this oatmeal. It wasn't the thick kind because we didn't have a whole lot and she had four kids to feed. So she made it very thin and poured it in a jar with butter, milk, and sugar. We would drink it hot, snuggled down between those sheets.

The coldness outside and the warmth of the oatmeal inside—it was just amazing.

My grandmother was the sweetest lady. Her name was Sally Knight. She favored my baby brother, David. This is the honest truth: She would cook fried chicken for that boy every single day. That was his favorite food and nobody else was allowed to touch it. I told that boy, "One day you gonna grow up and cluck." That's how much chicken he ate. She got cancer and was in the hospital. Well, David—he was playing ball and he got nicked on the head—so he went to the hospital too. He came in to see Grandma and she looked at David, and yelled: "Y'all ain't taking care of my baby. What is wrong with his head?" Oh, she went off. Even on the day before she died, she was carrying on about her babies.

My dad said, "You're staying with your mother because that's where you should be. It's not that I don't love you, not that I don't want you, but you need your mom."

My parents showed lots of affection, but eventually they divorced. I was eleven. At that point, you could see that they weren't happy anymore. I didn't feel it was my fault. My mom and my dad were the kinds of parents who didn't make us feel we had to choose between the two. My dad said, "You're staying with your mother because that's where you should be. It's not that I don't love you, not that I don't want you, but you need your mom." And my mom said, "You have total access to your father any time you want to see him." After we grew up and got to the point where we could ride the bus by ourselves, we'd just hop on the bus after school and go down to where my dad worked, hang out with him, come on back home. Matter of fact, my brother ended up working at the same store with my dad, so it wasn't like we were totally cut off from either parent.

I'm grateful for every episode in my life—good and bad. I don't look back and say, "I wish I could do this or I wish I could do that." There are certain aches and pains that maybe I wouldn't want to revisit—but were it not for those aches and pains, I wouldn't be where I am today.

candice bergen

I wanted to be a cowgirl. And when I got a little older, I wanted to be Brenda Starr. She was the star of a comic strip in the newspapers, a newspaper reporter with red hair and stars flashing in her eyes. She had a phantom mystery man named Basil St. John who sent her black orchids from the Amazonian rain forest. A black orchid arrived, and that's how you knew Basil was back.

I wanted to be a cowgirl.

> I wish I were supernaturally strong
> so I could put **right** everything
> that is wrong.
>
> —**Greta Garbo**

lisa leslie

When I was a girl, I thought I would grow up to be a weather reporter. I just thought that was going to be the best thing for me—to be in front of the camera. At the time, that was a great job for a woman to have—at least, it seemed to me.

sandra bernhard

I dreamed of being a superstar diva, a Broadway musical comedy songstress, a sophisticate, an international supermodel—everything that I turned out to be.

I dreamed of being a superstar diva.

candace bushnell

I never really thought about doing anything but writing, and I didn't understand people who didn't know what they wanted to do. I thought that was strange.

ann curry

I remember in about fifth grade wanting to be an astronaut and then being told that only boys were astronauts and, in fact, only boys were astronauts at that time. Then I thought I might want to be a nurse, because girls were nurses. Then the women's movement happened. Growing up at a time when women were marching in the streets and demanding equal rights. My goodness. I was being raised in one world and entering a new one.

Growing up at a time when women were marching in the streets and demanding equal rights.
My goodness.
I was being raised in one world and entering a new one.

My role model was Walter Cronkite. I couldn't ask for a better role model, but he wasn't a girl so it was difficult to imagine myself in that position. When I was graduating from high school, I thought I might want to do something in news. Having watched Walter Cronkite all those years, having felt—in our little town in Oregon— the importance of events happening thousands of miles away . . . that affected me. My father told me to be of service, and I thought I could be of service by providing knowledge, that this would be a way of doing good. That's why I chose to become a reporter.

I became a reporter, not for fame or fortune. Frankly, they weren't necessarily available when I became a reporter. I became a reporter because I wanted to make a difference. That sounds Pollyannaish but it's true.

edie falco

Applying to college, I thought I'd become a writer or a shrink. It really wasn't until a teacher who'd seen me in school plays suggested I check acting off as an interest on a college brochure that the idea crossed my mind. "So why don't you become an actress?" she said. Well, that was the most outrageous thing that I'd ever heard.

teri garr

I wanted to be in show business. It seemed to me that in show business, every day was like somebody's wedding. Dresses have to be fitted right, shoes all have names in them—it was so much better than real life.

Real life—where you have to carry your books and get on the bus—was dismal. I wanted to be in show business.

Real life—where you have to carry your books and get on the bus—was dismal. I wanted to be in show business.

anna quindlen

When I was a girl, I wanted to be a famous writer—that's what I wanted to be. If I could have narrowed it down I would have said I wanted to be Charles Dickens. I wanted to write big discursive novels that hundreds of thousands of people would buy.

It's strange, because of course I didn't know anyone who wrote for money. I don't think that I even really knew that you *could* write for money. The kinds of jobs our fathers had were very clear. They went to an office or they manufactured products; they were making widgets or selling widgets. The notion that you could manufacture words and that someone would pay for them never really occurred to me. I certainly never met anyone who was a writer. And yet somehow I just thought that was what I was going to do.

cherry jones

I wanted to be an actress. I don't ever remember wanting to be anything else. It was the only thing I seemed really good at. I wasn't particularly good in school. I got by, but that was it.

sally ride

when i was a girl ...

I grew up in a suburb of Los Angeles, a typical middle-class suburban neighborhood. My father was a teacher in a local community college; my mother was a homemaker, and in the mid-fifties it was a very typical home. It wasn't quite *Leave It to Beaver*, but it had that sense about it. It was a very friendly suburban neighborhood—there were lots of families, lots of young kids, lots of playing on the streets.

I would say I was a combination of a happy kid and a shy kid. I was always interested in being outside, doing things, being active. Even at age five or six, I liked sports—although I wouldn't have known what sports were. I liked running around in the yard; I like playing with my friends; I liked just being out in the Southern California weather.

I was always looking up at the sky. At about seven or eight, I became fascinated with the planets and the stars. I asked my parents for a telescope before I knew what a telescope was. I got one of those old spyglass things. I'd look out and try to find the moon and try to find the planets.

I asked my parents for a telescope before I knew what a telescope was.

I didn't really think too much about what would it be like to walk on Venus, or be on Mars. I was much more focused on which star was which, what were they made of, how far away they were. My fantasies didn't really include people or living spaces on other worlds, or colonies in space. All kids are really natural scientists, and it's just a question of what it is that they're curious about and what they wonder about.

I thought I would grow up to become a scientist—either that, or a baseball player. I loved playing baseball out on the street with friends in the neighborhood. When I was too young to know that women couldn't play for the Dodgers, I wanted to be their shortstop. My father told me that that was probably not the appropriate career choice for his young daughter, so I started thinking more seriously about science. He explained to me that I could still keep playing baseball, that I could still play with my friends, but as a career it seemed far off. Perhaps I couldn't play short-stop for the Dodgers, but I could do what I wanted to do.

When I was girl, I thought my mother was the smartest person alive. She seemed to know the answer to every question. She was not a scientist; she was not a professional in any way. But any time I had a question, she seemed to know the answer to it. My parents wanted me to be exposed to many things. If I was interested in science, then I should pur-sue that; if I was interested in tennis, I should play tennis. There really weren't significant limitations put on me. My parents didn't seem to have preconceptions about what either my sister or I should do or become—at least if they did, they didn't let us know what those were. Both my mother and father were very supportive of my interests.

I was a very good tennis player. I played on the circuit, and for a few moments made a career in tennis a short-term goal. I was playing in a tennis tournament in Wilmington, Delaware, the day Neil Armstrong set foot on the moon. I was staying with a friend on the tennis circuit, at the home of people belonging to the country club where the tennis tournament was being played. We watched the moon landing from the den of their house and were just glued to the television. I remember that day as clearly as if it were yesterday—as do, I think, most people who were growing up at that time. This was the first time that anyone from Earth had set foot on any other moon or planet in the solar system. It was our first real venture to another world, and we all felt it. I think it gave our generation a special bond.

Going into high school, I knew that I was fascinated by science, I knew that I really liked math, I knew that those were the subjects that interested me most. But I was living for the moment, not aiming for a career. I had two teachers in high school—both female and both science teachers—whom I admired very much. One was a young chemistry teacher who was probably twenty-three or twenty-four, just out of college; the other was an older, very accomplished woman, with a Ph.D. who taught physiology. She would present problems that were almost puzzles and games, brain twisters that we were encouraged to try to take several days to solve, and I really got into it, I was totally captivated by it. Solving these twisters was a great feeling of accomplishment. Knowing I had a brain that could make logical sense of problems, that could find solutions—it gave me a real appreciation for the different contributions that different people can make to the world.

When I graduated from high school, I had no expectations of what was going to happen. I just kind of moved along.

When I graduated from high school, I had no expectations of what was going to hap-

SALLY RIDE

pen. I just kind of moved along. I've never been a particularly goal-oriented person. Getting a Ph.D. was a defining moment for me; knowing I'd done something I'd carry along with me for my entire life definitely changed me. But it wasn't until I landed from my first trip into space that I appreciated the importance of what I had accomplished.

All these women came up to me and told me how proud they were that the world had changed, how they wished they'd been born thirty years later so that they could fulfill their dreams. But probably what was most rewarding was having little eleven-year-old girls tell me that they wanted to be astronauts when they grew up. It was as if it had never occurred to them that they couldn't. They could see that once I was a little girl who was able to do something they wanted to do.

when i

was

a

woman

It is never too late

to be

what you

might have been.

—George Eliot

edie **falco**

I never ever would have imagined my life could feel as good as it does now.

anna quindlen

Starting out, if she's lucky, a girl has it all: moxy, lack of fear, understanding of human relationships. It's the world that tries to tone her down, have her go a little this way and a little that way. You look at a four-year-old girl when she's pissed off, with her fists on those little hipless hips and fire in her eyes, and you think, *Oh, yeah, that's what real anger looks like.* I remember myself at that age and think, *That girl had the potential to do everything she needed to do.*

melanie griffith

What do I miss about being a girl? How tight my
body was! Other than that, nothing. I think God just
made a little mistake. He should have reversed it. We
should be born really old and saggy, bald and fat and
ugly. Then, as you get older, you should start looking
younger and younger. By the time you're eighty,
you're back in the crib! That would be cool.

jo dee messina

I miss not having to worry. It breaks my heart to see
kids worrying, because for me childhood was a time
to dream, to be free, to float through life, to walk in
the clouds. It's funny, now when I look back at pictures, I think *I didn't realize my furniture was all
ripped up.* I didn't realize the front door didn't have
paint on it or the rug was filled with holes. I didn't
know that my mother was worrying about putting the
next meal on the table. I didn't realize she was worrying about the next paycheck. I didn't have a lot as a
kid, but I had love and encouragement.

candace bushnell

If I could relive any moment from my childhood, it'd probably be when I won a blue ribbon at a horse show. I was at this pretty big event in Vermont and I just knew I was going to win. From the beginning, I knew I was going to win. It was that amazing feeling of flow.

kathy najimy

When I was a girl, I had such a burden on my shoulders. I don't miss the uneasiness. I don't miss being uncomfortable in my body. I remember we had to go to a funeral once and I must have been about fourteen and we had to buy a dark suit. That was one of the most traumatic experiences in my life—finding a suit that fit—and then there were those nylon stockings that rubbed together, so your legs were sweaty and horrible and the crotch would be down by your knees. Feeling so uncomfortable in my own body, I don't miss that. And, thankfully, I don't spend a minute in that land anymore.

You're ten and you wake up on a Saturday with no responsibilities, and it's summer and glorious out.

But I do sometimes miss that feeling of the day being the longest day in the world. You're ten and you wake up on a Saturday with no responsibilities, and it's summer and glorious out.

Now, my favorite vacation is to get in the car with my husband, my daughter, and my dogs and have no plan. You are not meeting anyone, you don't have a reservation at a hotel, you don't have to look a certain way. And we get in the car and we drive. Wherever we want to go is where we end up. And that's the closest I can get to recapturing those days.

jane pratt

I miss that sense that everything is okay. I miss that lying in the backseat while your parents are driving and talking and you can't hear what they are saying, but you just hear those voices. You feel so relaxed and safe and you just fall asleep. I want that back.

I miss that lying in the backseat while your parents are driving and talking and you can't hear what they are saying, but you just hear those voices. You feel so relaxed and safe and you just fall asleep. I want that back.

I'm still a girl, really, in pretty much every way. I only recently became comfortable being a woman. Even the way I dress—I dress myself like a girl. My fingernails are short and bitten off. And I still love Sugar Daddies. My taste is very much the same way it was when I was ten years old and I painted my room green and blue.

joan chen

I miss the feeling of waiting. I felt a lot of expectation and anticipation when I was a girl. Like, we'd wait for the beginning of every month when the salaries came in, because then we'd get a certain meal. Now, I make a meal I treasured back then and wonder, *Maybe this is not cooked right.* Because it never tastes the same. But, really, it was all the anticipation, the expectation involved that made the food taste good. Waiting makes everything more romantic.

wendie malick

If I could tell my girlhood self something, I'd say, "Be mindful of the fact that each day is one that will never come again, so don't rush through it. Savor it."

sally ride

The experience of a launch is a combination of exhilarating, terrifying, and overwhelming all just smashed into eight electrifying minutes. The first time that I looked out the window of the shuttle and had a minute to look back at Earth, it was just a very rewarding experience. To see our planet just hanging out there in the middle of space; I appreciated for the first time that I lived on good solid ground, breathed the air. Seeing that your house, your neighborhood, your city are all on this orbiting ball of rock out there in the middle of a solar system going around the sun, protected from this emptiness and coldness and vacuum of space.

The experience of a launch is a combination of exhilarating, terrifying, and overwhelming all just smashed into eight electrifying minutes.

The earth's atmosphere is really very, very thin and that's all that protects us from the total emptiness of space; it puts the world in a new context and gives you a real appreciation for the fragility of the planet and the civilizations that have developed over the ages. It just puts everything in a much larger context.

ALISON POLLET lives in New York City. She is working on a novel for middle-grade readers to be published by Orchard Books/Scholastic in Fall 2004.